Cambridge Elements ≡

Elements in the Philosophy of Mathematics
edited by
Penelope Rush
University of Tasmania
Stewart Shapiro
The Ohio State University

MATHEMATICAL PLURALISM

Graham Priest
City University of New York
University of Melbourne
Ruhr University of Bochum

CAMBRIDGE
UNIVERSITY PRESS

CAMBRIDGE
UNIVERSITY PRESS

Shaftesbury Road, Cambridge CB2 8EA, United Kingdom

One Liberty Plaza, 20th Floor, New York, NY 10006, USA

477 Williamstown Road, Port Melbourne, VIC 3207, Australia

314–321, 3rd Floor, Plot 3, Splendor Forum, Jasola District Centre, New Delhi – 110025, India

103 Penang Road, #05–06/07, Visioncrest Commercial, Singapore 238467

Cambridge University Press is part of Cambridge University Press & Assessment, a department of the University of Cambridge.

We share the University's mission to contribute to society through the pursuit of education, learning and research at the highest international levels of excellence.

www.cambridge.org
Information on this title: www.cambridge.org/9781009500968

DOI: 10.1017/9781009091640

First published 2024

A catalogue record for this publication is available from the British Library.

ISBN 978-1-009-50096-8 Hardback
ISBN 978-1-009-09541-9 Paperback
ISSN 2399-2883 (online)
ISSN 2514-3808 (print)

Mathematical Pluralism

Elements in the Philosophy of Mathematics

DOI: 10.1017/9781009091640
First published online: March 2024

Graham Priest
City University of New York
University of Melbourne
Ruhr University of Bochum

Author for correspondence: Graham Priest, priest.graham@gmail.com

Abstract: Mathematical pluralism is the view that there is an irreducible plurality of pure mathematical structures, each with its own internal logics, and that qua pure mathematical structures they are all equally legitimate. Mathematical pluralism is a relatively new position on the philosophical landscape. This Element provides an introduction to the position.

Keywords: mathematical pluralism, mathematical foundationalism, mathematical objects, applied mathematics, non-classical logic

ISBNs: 9781009500968 (HB), 9781009095419 (PB), 9781009091640 (OC)
ISSNs: 2399-2883 (online), 2514-3808 (print)

Contents

Foreword

Since I came to philosophy from mathematics, my first philosophical love was the philosophy of mathematics. I have acquired many other philosophical interests since then; but I have never lost a philosophical interest, and every new interest makes the old interests richer. So it is that I have regularly returned to the philosophy of mathematics, seeing old issues in new lights. In fact, over the years, I think my views on the philosophy of mathematics have changed more than those concerning any other area of philosophy. I was never sympathetic to platonism;[1] but the landscape of the philosophy of mathematics (to say nothing of the rest of philosophy) has changed substantially in the last 50 years, and (it seems to me) there are now much better ways of framing an anti-platonist view.

In particular, over the last 10 years or so I have become sympathetic to mathematical pluralism. So when Penny Rush and Stewart Shapiro approached me to write a short Element on the topic in their Philosophy of Mathematics *Cambridge Elements* Series, I was very happy to accept. This provided a welcome opportunity to attempt to weld a number of things I have written on the topic in the last few years into a (hopefully!) coherent whole. These are referenced in what follows.[2] Section 1 largely reproduces Priest (2019a), and Section 3 largely reproduces Priest (202+a). I am grateful to the editors and publishers of those pieces for permission to reuse the material.

Many thanks go to a number of friends who, in commenting on earlier drafts of the manuscript, parts thereof, or in conversation, gave me valuable thoughts and criticisms. These include Justin Clarke-Doane, Hartry Field, Will Nava, Lavinia Picollo, Andrew Tedder, and Elia Zardini. Thanks go to Joel Hamkins for technical help on set theory. I taught a course on the philosophy of mathematics at the CUNY Graduate Center in the Spring semester, 2022, where my students read (amongst other things) a draft manuscript and gave me valuable comments and criticisms. Many thanks go to them too. A special thanks goes to Stewart Shapiro. Stewart read what I expected to be essentially the final draft of the manuscript, and his perceptive comments and suggestions led to the current improved version.

---

[1] As can be seen from Priest (1973).

[2] My first foray into the area was Priest (2013a).

Preface

One may hold there to be a unity to mathematics; that is, that there is one overarching framework into which all of (true) mathematics fits. I doubt that one finds this view in the history of mathematics before the twentieth century. At least before Descartes, there was a pretty rigid distinction between arithmetic (the investigations of numbers) and geometry (the investigation of spatial relations). And after the invention/discovery of non-Euclidean geometries, there was, I think, no sense that they could all be subsumed under a unifying framework before Riemann.

In the twentieth century, the view that there was such a unity to mathematics did, however, become orthodox. The unifying framework was that of Zermelo–Fraenkel set theory – usually, with the Axiom of Choice – *ZFC*. That *ZFC* played this role emerged from studies in the foundations of mathematics in the late nineteenth and early twentieth centuries. As one highly respected philosopher of mathematics, Penelope Maddy, describes this moment in the history of mathematics/philosophy:[3]

> The view of set theory as a foundation for mathematics emerged early in the thinking of the originators of the theory and is now a pillar of contemporary orthodoxy. As such, it is enshrined in the opening pages of most recent textbooks; to take a few illustrative examples:
>
> *All branches of mathematics are developed, consciously or unconsciously, in set theory. (Levy (1979), 3)*
>
> *Set theory is the foundation of mathematics. All mathematical concepts are defined in terms of the primitive notions of set and membership . . . From [the] axioms, all known mathematics may be derived. (Kunen (1980), xi)*
>
> *[M]athematical objects (such as numbers and differentiable functions) can be defined to be certain sets. And the theorems of mathematics (such as the fundamental theorem of calculus) then can be viewed as statements about sets. Furthermore, these theorems will be provable from our axioms. Hence, our axioms provide a sufficient collection of assumptions for the development of the whole of mathematics – a remarkable fact. (Enderton (1977), 10–11)*
>
> From its Cantorian beginnings through its modern flowerings, set theory has also raised problems of its own, like any other branch of mathematics, but its larger, foundational role has been and remains conspicuous and distinctive.

What it means to say that a theory is foundational for mathematics is no straightforward matter, and different philosophers have held somewhat

---

[3] Maddy (1997), p. 22.

different views on the matter. Maddy discusses various possible interpretations of the view: ontological, epistemological, and methodological. But the details here need not concern us.[4] However one understands what, exactly, it amounts to, *ZFC* is taken to be a single framework into which all of mathematics, in some sense, fits. As Maddy herself summarises matters:[5]

> Finally, perhaps most fundamentally, *this single, unified arena for mathematics* provides a court of final appeal for questions of mathematical existence and proof: if you want to know if there is a mathematical object of a certain sort, you ask (ultimately) if there is a set theoretic surrogate of that sort; if you want to know if a given statement is provable or disprovable, you mean (ultimately), from the axioms of the theory of sets.

And again:[6]

> set theoretic foundations ... *play a strong unifying role*: vague structures are made more precise, old theorems are given new proofs and *unified with other theorems* that previously seemed quite distinct, similar hypotheses are traced at the basis of disparate mathematical fields, existence questions are given explicit meaning, unprovable conjectures can be identified, new hypotheses can settle old open questions, and so on. That set theory plays this role is central to modern mathematics, that it is able to play this role is perhaps the most remarkable outcome of the search for foundations.

That there is a unity to mathematics became, as she says, the orthodox view amongst philosophers of mathematics in the twentieth century. Arguably, it still is.[7]

However, the view is now starting to give way to one according to which there is no such unity. Mathematics is irreducibly a plurality. There is no grand narrative into which it can all be fitted. Indeed, it is investigations into the area of the foundations of mathematics which have themselves brought the view to breaking point.

One may call the emerging view, naturally enough, *mathematical pluralism*, and the point of this Element is to explain and examine the view. It is no impartial guide, however. It also endorses and argues for the view. It is none

---

[4] For one clear discussion of the matter, see Shapiro (2004).

[5] Maddy (1997), p. 26. My italics in this and the next quotation.

[6] Maddy (1997), p. 34 f.

[7] In a later publication Maddy reiterates her position, though she restricts it, without much explanation, to 'classical' mathematics (Maddy (2007), p. 354). What she means by 'classical mathematics' is not entirely clear; but if it means mathematics based on classical logic, even this more restricted claim runs aground on classical mathematical theories that do not fit into *ZFC*, as we will note in 2.2.

the worse, I think, for that. New views need advocates to make their full force felt. Orthodoxy will never lack its conservative defenders.

In Section 1, we will look at the evolution of studies in the foundations of mathematics in the twentieth century, and see how mathematical pluralism arose naturally out of these. Then in Section 2, we will have a closer look at mathematical pluralism itself, some of its features, and some possible objections.

The mathematics I have been talking about and which is discussed in the first two sections is pure mathematics. But mathematics also encompasses applied mathematics. What is one to make of this on a pluralist view? Section 3 investigates. Unsurprisingly, the picture which emerges is different from that which normally goes with set-theoretic foundationalism.

As hardly needs to be said, the nature of mathematics is deeply entangled with the nature of logic. Here is not the place to discuss all matters involved in the bearing of mathematical pluralism on that topic. However, the last section in the Element, Section 4, discusses what I take to be some of the most important issues.

Of course, in an Element of this length it is inevitable that a number of important issues receive no more than a cursory discussion. However, by the end of our short journey through the terrain of mathematical pluralism, you, the reader, will, I hope, have a decent understanding of the view and its features. What to make of it is, as ever in philosophy, up to you to decide.

> *Indeed, even at this stage, I predict a time when*
> *there will be mathematical investigations of calculi*
> *containing contradictions, and people will actually*
> *be proud of having emancipated themselves*
> *from consistency.*
> Wittgenstein (1964), p. 332. (Written in 1930.)

1 From the Foundations of Mathematics to Mathematical Pluralism

1.1 Introduction

I think that an illuminating way of understanding contemporary mathematical pluralism is to see how it has come about. As I indicated in the preface, it has done so as a result of studies in the so-called foundations of mathematics and the problems this has exposed in the attempt to find such a foundation. In this section I will review this story.

For the most part, the story is well known. Where this is so, I shall just give some standard reference to the material at the end of each section.[8] When, towards the end of the section, we move to material that is not so well known, I will give fuller references.

1.2 A Century of Mathematical Rigour

Let us start by winding the clock back to the end of the nineteenth century. The nineteenth century may be fairly thought of as the age of mathematical rigour, in a certain sense. At the start of the century, many species in the genus of number were well known: natural numbers, rational numbers, real numbers, negative numbers, complex numbers, infinitesimals; but many aspects of them and their behaviour were not well understood. Equations could have imaginary roots; but what exactly is an imaginary number? Infinitesimals were essential to the computation of integrals and derivatives; but what were these 'ghosts of departed quantities', as Berkeley had put it?[9] The century was to clear up much of the obscurity.

Early in the century, the notion of a limit appeared in Cauchy's formulation of the calculus. Instead of considering what happens to a function when some infinitesimal change is made to an argument, one considers what happens when one makes a small finite change and then sees what happens 'in the limit', as that number approaches 0 (the limit being a number which may be approached

---

[8] A good general reference for the standard material is Hatcher (1982).
[9] *The Analyst, or a Discourse Addressed to an Infidel Mathematician* (1734), §XXXV.

as closely as one pleases, though never, perhaps, attained). Despite the fact that Cauchy possessed the notion of a limit, he mixed both infinitesimal and limit terminology. It was left to Weierstrass, later in the century, to replace all appeals to infinitesimals by appeals to limits. At this point, infinitesimals disappeared from the numerical menagerie – though they were later to make some comebacks in the forms of non-standard analysis and the theory of smooth infinitesimals, as we shall see.[10]

Weierstrass also gave the first modern account of negative numbers, defining them as signed reals, that is, pairs whose first members are reals, and whose second members are 'sign bits' ('+' or '−'), subject to suitable operations. A contemporary of Weierstrass, Tannery, gave the first modern account of rational numbers. He defined a rational number as an equivalence class of pairs of natural numbers, $\langle m, n \rangle$, where $n \neq 0$, under the equivalence relation, $\sim$, defined by

$$\langle m, n \rangle \sim \langle r, s \rangle \ \text{iff} \ m \cdot s = r \cdot n.$$

Earlier in the century, Gauss and Argand had shown how to think of complex numbers of the form $x + iy$ as points on the two-dimensional Euclidean plane – essentially as a pair of the form $\langle x, y \rangle$ – with the arithmetic operations defined in an appropriate fashion.

A rigorous analysis of real numbers was provided in different ways by Dedekind, Weierstrass, and Cantor. Weierstrass' analysis was in terms of infinite decimal expansions; Cantor's was in terms of infinite sequences of rationals which converge to each other. Dedekind's analysis was arguably the simplest. A *Dedekind section* is any partition of the rational numbers into two parts, $\langle L, R \rangle$, where for any $l \in L$ and $r \in R$, $l < r$. A real number can be thought of as a Dedekind section (or just its left-hand part).

So this is how things stood by late in the century. Every kind of number in extant mathematics – with the exception of infinitesimals, which had been abolished – had been reduced to simple set-theoretic constructions out of, in the last instance, natural numbers.

What, then, of the natural numbers themselves? Dedekind gave the first axiomatisation of these – essentially the now familiar Peano Axioms. This certainly helped to frame the question, but it did not answer it.[11]

1.3 Frege and the Natural Numbers

Which brings us to Frege. Frege was able to draw on the preceding developments, but he also defined the natural numbers in purely set-theoretic

---

[10] See Bell (2022).
[11] For the material in this section, see Priest (1998).

terms.[12] The natural number n was essentially the set of all n-membered sets (so that 0 is the set whose only member is the empty set, 1 is the set of all singletons, etc.) This might seem unacceptably circular, but Frege showed that circularity could be avoided, and indeed, how all the properties of numbers (as given by the Dedekind axioms) could be shown to follow from the appropriate definitions.

But 'follow from' how? The extant canons of logic – essentially a form of syllogistic – were not up to the job, as was pretty clear. Frege, then, had to develop a whole new canon of logic, his *Begriffsschrift*. Thus did Frege's work give birth to 'classical logic'.

Given Frege's constructions, all of the familiar numbers and their properties could now be shown to be sets of certain kinds. But what of sets themselves? Frege took these to be abstract (non-physical) objects satisfying what we would now think of as an unrestricted comprehension schema. Thus (in modern notation), any condition, $A(x)$, defines a set of objects $\{x : A(x)\}$. Because he was using second-order logic, Frege was able to define membership. Again in modern notation, $x \in y$ if and only if $\exists Z(y = \{z : Zz\} \wedge Zx)$.

Moreover, Frege took these set-theoretic principles themselves to be principles of pure logic. Hence all of arithmetic (that is, the theory of numbers) was a matter of pure logic – a view now called *logicism*. And this provided an answer to the question of how we may know the truths of arithmetic – or to be more precise, reduced it to the question of how we know the truths of logic. As to this, Frege assumed, in common with a well-worn tradition, that these were simply a priori.

Frege's achievement was spectacular. Unfortunately, as is well known, there was one small, but devastating, fly in the ointment, discovered by Russell. The naive comprehension principle was inconsistent. Merely take for $A(x)$ the condition that $x \notin x$, and we have the familiar Russell paradox. If B is the sentence $\{x : x \notin x\} \in \{x : x \notin x\}$ then $B \wedge \neg B$. Given the properties of classical logic, everything followed – a disaster.

After the discovery of Russell's paradox, Frege tried valiantly to rescue his program, but unsuccessfully. The next developments of the *Zeitgeist* were to come from elsewhere.[13]

1.4 Type Theory

Namely, Russell – and his partner in logical crime, Whitehead. Russell was also a logicist, but a more ambitious one than Frege. For him, *all* mathematics, and

---

[12] Strictly speaking, in terms of courses of values.

[13] For the material in this section, see Zalta (2016).

not just arithmetic, was to be logic. In the first instance, this required reducing the other traditional part of mathematics – geometry – to logic, as well. This was relegated to Volume IV of the mammoth *Principia Mathematica*, which never appeared.

But by this time, things were more complex than this. The work of Cantor on the infinite had generated some new kinds of numbers: transfinite ones. These were of two kinds, cardinals, measuring size, and ordinals, measuring order. Russell generalised Frege's definition of number to all cardinals: a cardinal number was *any* set containing all those sets between which there is a one-to-one correspondence. He generalised it further again to ordinals. An ordered set is *well-ordered* if every subset has a least member. An ordinal is any set containing all those well-ordered sets between which there is an order-isomorphism.

Of course, Russell still had to worry about his paradox, and others of a similar kind which, by that time, had multiplied. His solution was *type theory*. The precise details were complex and need not concern us here. Essentially, sets[14] were to be thought of as arranged in a hierarchy of types, such that quantifiers could range over one type only. Given a condition with a variable of type i, $A(x_i)$, comprehension delivered a set $\{x_i : A(x_i)\}$; this set, however, was not of type i, but of a higher type, and so it could not be substituted into the defining condition delivering Russell's paradox to produce contradiction.

Russell's construction faced a number of problems. For a start, it was hard to motivate the hierarchy of orders as a priori, and so as part of logic. Secondly, with his construction, Frege had been able to show that there were infinite sets (such as the set of natural numbers). The restrictions of type theory did not allow this proof. Russell therefore had to have an axiom to the effect that there was such a thing: the *Axiom of Infinity*. It was hard to see this as an a priori truth as well.[15]

On top of these, there were problems of a more technical nature. For a start, the hierarchy of types meant that the numbers were not unique: every type (at least, every type which was high enough) had its own set of numbers of each kind. This was, to say the least, ugly. Moreover, Cantor's work had delivered transfinite numbers of very large kinds. Type theory delivered only a small range of these. Specifically, if $\beth_0 = \aleph_0$, $\beth_{n+1} = 2^{\beth_n}$, and $\beth_\omega = \bigcup_{n<\omega} \beth_n$, then type theory delivered only those cardinals less than $\beth_\omega$. Of course, one could just deny that there were cardinals greater than these, but prima facie, they certainly seemed coherent.

---

[14] Or, strictly speaking, propositional functions.

[15] Earlier versions of type theory also required a somewhat problematic axiom called the *Axiom of Reducibility*. Subsequent simplifications of type theory showed how to avoid this.

Finally, to add insult to injury, one could not even explain type theory without quantifying over all sets, and so violating type restrictions.

Russell fought gallantly against these problems – unsuccessfully.[16]

1.5 ZF

New developments arrived at the hands of Zermelo. He proposed simply to axiomatise set theory. He would enunciate axioms that were strong enough to deliver the gains of the nineteenth-century foundational results, but not strong enough to run afoul of the paradoxes. His 1908 axiom system, strengthened a little by later thinkers, notably Fraenkel, appeared to do just this. The axioms were something of a motley, and so all hope of logicism seemed lost;[17] but, on the other hand, the system did not have the technical inadequacies of type theory.

The key to avoiding the paradoxes of set theory was to replace the naive comprehension schema with the *Aussonderung* principle. A condition, $A(x)$, was not guaranteed to define a set; but given any set, y, it defined the subset of y comprising those things satisfying $A(x)$. An immediate consequence of this was that there could be no set of all sets – or Russell's paradox would reappear. Indeed, all 'very large' sets of this kind had to be junked, but with a bit of fiddling, the mathematics of the day did not seem to need these.

In particular, the Frege/Russell cardinals and ordinals were just such large sets. So to reduce number theory to set theory, a different definition had to be found. Zermelo himself suggested one. Later orthodoxy was to prefer a somewhat more elegant definition proposed by von Neumann. 0 is the empty set. $\alpha + 1$ is $\alpha \cup \{\alpha\}$, and given a set, X, of ordinals closed under successors, the ordinal which is the limit of these is $\bigcup X$. A cardinal was an ordinal such that there was no smaller ordinal that could be put in one-to-one correspondence with it.

Logicism had died. The fruits of nineteenth-century reductionism had been preserved. The paradoxes had been avoided. The cost was eschewing all 'large' sets, but this seemed to be a price worth paying. The next developments came from a quite different direction.[18]

---

[16] Starting around the 1990s, there was a logicist revival of sorts, neo-logicism; but it never delivered the results hoped of it. For the material in this section, see Irvine (2015) and Tennant (2017).

[17] About 20 years later, in the work of von Neumann and Zermelo, a model of sorts was found: the cumulative hierarchy. This did provide more coherence for the axioms, but it did nothing to save logicism. On the contrary, it appeared to give set theory a distinctive non-logical subject matter.

[18] For the material in this section, see Hallett (2013).

1.6 Intuitionism

In the first 20 years of the twentieth century, Brouwer rejected the idea that mathematical objects were abstract objects of a certain kind: he held them to be mental objects. Such an object exists, then, only when there is some mental procedure for constructing it (at least in principle). In mathematics, then, existence is constructibility. Brouwer took his inspiration from Kant. Mental constructions occur in time. Time, according to Kant, is a mental faculty which enforms sensations – or intuitions, as Kant called them. Hence, Brouwer's view came to be called *Intuitionism*. Intuitionism provides a quite different answer from that provided by logicism as to how we know the truths of mathematics: we know them in the way that we know the workings of our own mind (whatever that is).

Brouwer's metaphysical picture had immediate logical consequences. Suppose that we want to show that $\exists x A(x)$. We assume, for reductio, that $\neg \exists x A(x)$, and deduce a contradiction. This shows that $\neg\neg \exists x A(x)$; but this does not provide us with a way of constructing an object satisfying $A(x)$. Hence, it does now establish that $\exists x A(x)$. The Law of Double Negation (in one direction), then, fails. Nor is this the only standard principle of logic to fail. Suppose that the Principle of Excluded Middle (PEM) holds: $\exists x A(x) \vee \neg \exists x A(x)$. In the situation just envisaged, we have shown that $\neg\neg \exists x A(x)$, ruling out the second disjunct. Hence $\exists x A(x)$; but we still have no construction of an object satisfying $A(x)$. So this is not true. The PEM must fail.

Brouwer did not believe in formalising logical inference: mental processes, he thought, could not be reduced to anything so algorithmic. But a decade or so later, intuitionist logic was formalised by Heyting and others. Unsurprisingly, it turned out to be a logic considerably weaker than 'classical logic', rejecting, as it did, Excluded Middle, Double Negation, and other related principles.

Given the unacceptability of many classical forms of inference, Brouwer set about reworking the mathematics of his day. All proofs which did not meet intuitionistically acceptable standards had to be rejected. In some cases it was possible to find a proof of the same thing which was acceptable, but in many cases, not. Thus, for example, consider König's Lemma: every infinite tree with finite branching has at least one infinite branch. Such a branch may be thought of as a function, f, from the natural numbers to nodes of the branch, such that $f(0)$ is the root of the tree, and for all $n, f(n + 1)$ is an immediate descendant of $f(n)$. We may construct f as follows. The function $f(0)$ has an infinite number of descendants by supposition. We then run down the tree preserving this property, thus defining an infinite branch. Suppose that $f(n)$ has an infinite number of descendants. Since it has only a finite number of immediate descendants, at least one of these must have an infinite number of descendants. Let $f(n + 1)$ be one of these. The problem with this proof intuitionistically is that we have, in general, no way of knowing which node or nodes these are, so we have no construction which defines the next value of the function. There is, then, no such function, since we have no way of constructing it.

Brouwer delivered ingenious constructions, which were intuitionistically valid and could do some of the things that classically valid constructions could do. Thus, in the case of König's Lemma, he established something called the *Fan Theorem*. However, it was impossible to prove everything which had a classical proof. Intuitionistic mathematics was therefore essentially revisionary. There are things which can be established classically which have no intuitionist proof.

This may make it sound as though intuitionist mathematics is a proper part of classical mathematics. This, however, is not the case. True, not every proof that is classically valid is intuitionistically valid. But that means that there can be things which are inconsistent from a classical point of view, which are not so from an intuitionistic point of view. And this allows for the possibility that one may prove intuitionistically some things that are *not* valid in classical mathematics.

Take, for example, the theory of real numbers. Let U be the real numbers between 0 and 1; and think of these as functions from natural numbers to $\{1, 0\}$. Now consider a one-place function, F, from U to U. To construct F, we need to have a procedure which, given an input of F, f, defines its output, $F(f)$. And this means that for any n, we must have a way of defining $[F(f)](n)$. Since this must be an effective procedure, $[F(f)](n)$ must be determined by some 'initial segment' of f – that is, $\{f(i): i \leq m\}$ for some m. Hence, if f' agrees with f on this initial segment, $[F(f)](n)$ and $[F(f')](n)$ must be the same. It follows that $F(f)$ and $F(f')$ can be made as close as we please by making f and f' close enough. That is, all functions of the kind in question are continuous. This is simply false in classical real number theory: there are plenty of discontinuous functions. Intuitionism is not, then, simply that sub-part of classical mathematics which can be obtained by constructive means: it is sui generis.[19]

Ingenious though it was, though, intuitionist mathematics never really caught on in the general mathematical community. Mathematicians who did not accept Brouwer's philosophical leanings could see nothing wrong with the standard mathematics. Or perhaps more accurately, mathematicians were very

---

[19] Though one can, of course, simply consider the constructive part of classical mathematics. See Bridges (2013).

much wedded to this mathematics and so rejected Brouwer's philosophical leanings.[20]

1.7 Hilbert's Program

The suspicion of classical reasoning was not restricted just to intuitionists, though. It was shared by Hilbert, who was as classical as they came. The discovery of Russell's paradox, and the apparently a priori principles that lead to it, was still something of a shock to the mathematical community, and Hilbert wanted a safeguard against things of this kind happening again. This inaugurated what was to become known as *Hilbert's Program.*

Hilbert wanted to *prove* that this could not happen. Of course, the proof had to be a mathematical one; and to prove anything mathematical about something, one has to have a precise fix on it. Hence, the first part of the program required such a fix on mathematics or its various parts. This would be provided, Hilbert thought, by appropriate axiomatisations. Hilbert had already provided an axiom system for Euclidean geometry. So the next target for axiomatisation was arithmetic. The axiomatisation was to be based on classical logic – or at least the first-order part of Frege's logic, which Hilbert and his school cleaned up, giving the first really contemporary account of this.

Given the axiomatised arithmetic, this was then to be proved consistent. Of course, given that the proof of consistency was to be a mathematical one, and the security of mathematical reasoning was exactly what was at stake in the project, there was an immediate issue. If our mathematical tools are themselves inconsistent, maybe they can prove their own consistency. Indeed, given that classical logic is being employed, if arithmetic is inconsistent, it can prove anything.

Hilbert's solution was to insist that the reasoning involved in a consistency proof be of a very simple and secure kind. He termed this *finitary.* Exactly what finitary reasoning was, was never defined exactly, as far as I am aware; but it certainly was even weaker than the constructive reasoning of intuitionists. The danger of contradiction, it seemed to Hilbert, arose only when the infinite reared essentially its enticing but dangerous head. Hence the reasoning of the consistency proof had to be something like simple finite combinatorial reasoning – most notably, symbol-manipulation.

This approach allowed a certain philosophical perspective. Take the standard language of arithmetic. Numerals are constituted by '0' followed by some number of occurrences of the successor symbol. Terms are composed from

---

[20] Further on all these things, see Iemhoff (2013).

numerals recursively by applying the symbols for addition and multiplication. Equations are identities between terms. The Δ_0 fragment of the language is the closure of the equations under truth functions and bounded quantifiers (i.e., particular or universal quantifiers bounded by some particular number). The truth value of any Δ_0 statement can be determined in a finitary way. Terms can be reduced to numerals by the recursive definitions of addition and multiplication. Identities between numerals can be decided by counting occurrences of the successor symbol, and then truth functions do the rest, the bounded quantifiers being essentially finite conjunctions and disjunctions. So, according to Hilbert, we may take the Δ_0 statements to be the truly meaningful (contentful) part of arithmetic.

But what about the other statements? Given some axiom system for arithmetic, this will contain the finitary proofs of the true Δ_0 statements, but proofs will go well beyond this – notably, establishing statements with unbounded quantifiers. However, since the true Δ_0 statements are complete (that is, for any such statement, either it or its negation is true), the system is consistent if and only if it is a conservative extension of that fragment.[21] Thus, if the system is consistent, reasoning deploying statements not in the Δ_0 fragment can prove nothing new of this form. However, the statements might well have an instrumental value, in that using them can produce simpler and more expeditious proofs of Δ_0 statements. Hence, thought Hilbert, the non-Δ_0 sentences could be thought of as 'ideal elements' of our reasoning – in much the same way that postulating an ideal 'point at infinity' can do the same for proofs about finite points, or imaginary numbers can do the same for proofs about real numbers.[22]

The demise of Hilbert's Program is so well known that it hardly needs detailed telling. A young Gödel showed that any axiomatisation of arithmetic of sufficient power – at least one that is consistent – must be incomplete. That is, there will be statements, A, such that neither A nor $\neg A$ is provable. Since (classically) one of these must be true, there was no complete axiomatisation of arithmetic. Putting another nail in the coffin of the Program, Gödel also established that given such a system, there is a purely arithmetic statement which can naturally be thought of as expressing its consistency. However,

---

[21] If the system is not a conservative extension, it proves the negation of some true Δ_0 sentence, and so the system is inconsistent. Conversely, if it is inconsistent, since it can prove everything, it is not a conservative extension.

[22] In these cases, the ideal elements are not statements, but objects. Hilbert discovered that quantifiers could be eliminated by the use of his ε-symbol. Thus, $\exists x A(x)$ is equivalent to $A(\varepsilon x A(x))$. One might – though I don't think Hilbert ever suggested this – take ε-terms themselves to signify ideal objects. In this way non-Δ_0 statements might be thought of as statements of Δ_0 form, but which concern these ideal objects (as well as, possibly, real ones).

this is not provable within the system – again if it is consistent. Since the system encodes all finitary reasoning (and much more), this seemed to show that a finitary proof of the consistency of even this incomplete system was impossible.[23]

1.8 Category Theory

So, by mid-century, this is how things stood: apart from some rearguard actions, the great foundational programs of the first part of the twentieth century were defunct. This, however, was not an end of the matter. New developments were to come from a quite new branch of mathematics: category theory.

It is common in mathematics to consider classes of structures of a certain kind: groups, topological spaces, and so on. Important information about their common structure is delivered by the morphisms (structure-preserving maps) between them. When the range of one morphism is the domain of another, such morphisms can be composed. If we write composition as ∘, then the morphism $f \circ g$ is a map which, when applied to an object x, delivers the object obtained by applying f to $g(x)$.

Starting in the late 1940s, Eilenberg and MacLane generalised this way of looking at things, to deliver the notion of a category. The idea was taken up and developed substantially by later mathematicians, including Grothendieck and Lawvere.

A category is a bunch of objects, together with functions between them, thought of as morphisms, and often termed *arrows*, because of the way they are depicted diagrammatically. In fact, the objects may be dispensed with, since each may be identified with the identity function on it (which is a morphism). So the notion of a category may be axiomatised with a number of axioms concerning functional composition. A category is, then, any model of this axiom system (in the same way that a group, e.g., is any model of the axioms of the theory of groups). Hence, there is a category of all groups, all topological spaces, all sets, and so on. The category of a particular kind of structures (e.g., sets) may justify further axioms concerning functional composition, in the same way that a consideration of Abelian groups justifies axioms additional to those of groups in general.

But foundationally there is now a problem. Since the consolidation of set theory in the early part of the century, it had been assumed that all mathematics (ignoring intuitionist mathematics) could be formulated within set theory. One can, indeed, think naturally of a category as a set of a certain kind. But the

---

[23] For the material in this section, see Zach (2013).

problem is that categories such as those of all groups, all topological spaces, all sets – large categories, as they are called – are of the very large kind that had been excised from set theory by Zermelo in order to avoid Russell's paradox. It would seem, then, that set theory cannot provide any kind of foundation for category theory.

There are certain remedial measures one might essay. A large category is not a set, but one can think of it as a proper class (that is, collections that are 'too big' to be a member of any other collection), in the sense of NBG set theory (a weak form of second-order ZF) – proper classes being, in effect, sub-collections of sets which are not themselves members of anything. However, this is not generally good enough. For category theorists consider not only particular categories, but the category of functions between them. (Given two categories, the category of morphisms between them is called the *functor category*.) This is 'too big' even to be a proper class.

One solution to these problems is to deploy the 'Grothendieck hierarchy'. This is the cumulative hierarchy, with levels, V_α, for every ordinal α, together with the assumption that there are arbitrarily large inaccessible cardinals. As is well known, if ϑ is an inaccessible cardinal, V_ϑ is a model of ZF set theory, so all the usual set theoretic operations can be performed within it. We may then think of the categories of all sets, groups, and so on, as categories of objects in a V_ϑ. The categories themselves, their functor categories, and so on, are not in V_ϑ, but are denizens of higher levels of the cumulative hierarchy. Category theory, then, must be thought of as 'typically ambiguous', applying schematically to each V_ϑ.

The retrograde nature of this move is clear. The point of category theory is to chart commonalities of structure between *all* structures of a certain kind. The Grothendieck hierarchy explicitly reneges on this. One way to bring the point home is as follows. Suppose that we are considering a category of a certain kind, and we prove something of the form $\exists!x\forall y R(x,y)$. This might be some sort of representational theorem. Interpreting this at each level of the Grothendieck hierarchy, the uniqueness of the x in question is lost: all we have is one at every level.

An honest approach to category theory would seem, then, to take it to be a sui generis branch of mathematics. Some have even gone so far as to suggest that it should be taken as providing an adequate foundation for all mathematics, including set theory. The plausibility of this is delivered by the theory of *topoi*. Topoi are particularly powerful categories of a certain kind. (The category of all sets is one of them.) They can be characterised by adding further axioms concerning composition to the general axioms of category theory. All the standard constructions of set theory, at least all those which are involved in the reduction of the other normal parts of mathematics to set theory, can then be performed in a topos.

As a foundational strategy, the weakness of this move is evident. There are many topoi, and 'standard mathematics' can be reconstructed in each one. We are, thus, back to the theoretical reduplication which plagued type theory.

I think it fair to say that what to make of all these matters is still sub judice. However, we are still not at the end of our story.[24]

1.9 Paraconsistency

We have so far met two formal logics in the foregoing: classical and intuitionistic. In both of these, the principle of *Explosion* is valid: $A, \neg A \vdash B$, for all A and B. The inference might be thought of as 'vacuously valid' in these logics, since the premises can never hold in an interpretation. The principle is clearly counter-intuitive, though. Starting around the 1960s, the development of paraconsistent logic began, a *paraconsistent logic* being exactly one where Explosion is not valid. Using a paraconsistent logic we may therefore reason using inconsistent information in a perfectly sensible way. The information does not deliver triviality – that is, not everything can be established.

There are, in fact, many paraconsistent logics. Their key, semantically speaking, is to stop Explosion being vacuously valid by including in the domain of reasoning not only standard consistent situations, but also inconsistent ones. Thus, if p and q are distinct propositional parameters, there can be a situation where p and $\neg p$ hold, but q does not. This is not to suggest that these inconsistent situations may be actual. We reason, after all, about situations which are conjectural, hypothetical, and so on. However, the view that some of these inconsistent situations are actual (that is, that what holds in them is actually true) is called *dialetheism*.[25]

The possibility of employing a paraconsistent logic opens up new possibilities in a number of the foundational matters which we have met.[26] Thus, one of the possibilities that has been of much interest to paraconsistentists is set theory – and for obvious reasons: using a paraconsistent logic allows us to endorse the unrestricted comprehension schema. Contradictions such as Russell's paradox can be proved in the theory, but these are quarantined by the failure of Explosion. Moreover, it was proved that, with an appropriate

---

[24] For the material in this section, see Marquis (2014).

[25] On paraconsistency, see Priest, Tanaka, and Weber (2022). On dialetheism, see Priest, Berto, and Weber (2022).

[26] On inconsistent mathematics in general, see Mortensen (2017).

paraconsistent logic, naive set theory (that is, set theory with unrestricted comprehension) is non-trivial.[27]

This raises the prospect of regenerating Frege's foundational project. Of course, having an unrestricted comprehension schema does not guarantee that this project can be carried through. The set-theoretic principles are strong, but the logic is much weaker than classical logic. Things other than Explosion need to be given up. Notably, the principle of *Contraction*, $A \rightarrow (A \rightarrow B) \vdash A \rightarrow B$ cannot be endorsed, because of Curry's Paradox.[28]

It was only relatively recently that Weber was able to show that much of Frege's program *can* be carried out in such a theory.[29] He showed that many of the main results of cardinal and ordinal arithmetic can be proved in this set theory. Moreover, the theory can be used to prove the Axiom of Choice, as well as results that go beyond ZF set theory, such as the negation of the Continuum Hypothesis, and several large-cardinal principles. (Of course, in the context, this does not show that one cannot prove the negations of these as well.)

Weber's proofs have a couple of very distinctive elements. First, they use comprehension in a very strong form, namely:

$$\exists x \forall y \, (y \in x \leftrightarrow A)$$

where A may contain x itself. This provides the potential for having a fixed point, and so self-reference, built into the very characterisation of a set.[30] Next, Weber not only accommodates inconsistencies but makes constructive use of them. Thus, a number of the results concerning cardinality, such as Cantor's Theorem, make use of sets of the form $\{x \in X : r \in r\}$, where r is the set of all sets which are not members of themselves, and so inconsistent.

Whether Weber's proof methods, and the various distinctions they require one to draw are entirely unproblematic, is a question for further thought. Likewise, whether other aspects of set-theoretic reasonings (such as those required in model theory) can be obtained in naive set theory, requires further investigation.

Another of the foundational matters we have met, and with which paraconsistency engages, is that concerning Gödel's theorems. Gödel's first theorem is often glossed as saying that any 'sufficiently strong' axiomatic

---

[27] See Brady (1989).

[28] With naive comprehension we can define a set, c, such that $x \in c \leftrightarrow (x \in x \rightarrow \perp)$. Contraction and modus ponens then quickly deliver a proof of $\perp$.

[29] See Weber (2010) and (2012).

[30] Surprisingly, Brady's proof showed this strong form of comprehension to be non-trivial. Indeed, it was later noted by Petersen (2000), p. 383, fn 14, that under certain conditions the more restricted form of comprehension entails the stronger form. For proof and discussion, see Weber (2021), pp. 174–8.

theory of arithmetic is incomplete. In fact, what it shows is that it is either incomplete *or* inconsistent.[31] Of course, if inconsistency implies triviality, it is natural to ignore the second alternative. However, paraconsistency changes all that, since the theory may be complete, inconsistent, but non-trivial. (I note that there is nothing in the use of paraconsistent logic, as such, which problematises the proof of Gödel's theorem. The logic required of an arithmetic theory in order for it to hold is exceptionally minimal.)

Indeed, it is now known that there are paraconsistent axiomatic theories of arithmetic which contain all the sentences true in the standard model, and so which are complete (that is, for any sentence of the language, A, either A or $\neg A$ is in the theory). These theories are inconsistent, but non-trivial.[32] What foundational significance this has depends, of course, on the plausibility of the claim that arithmetic might be inconsistent.

Implausible as this may seem, Gödel's theorem itself might be thought to lead in this direction. At the heart of Gödel's proof of his theorem, there is a paradox. Consider the sentence 'this sentence is not provable'. If it is provable, it is true; so it is not provable. Hence it is not provable. But we have just proved this; so it is.

Of course, this argument cannot be carried through in a consistent arithmetic, such as classical Peano Arithmetic, when proof is understood as proof in that system. This may be a matter of relief; or it may just show the inadequacy of the system to encode perfectly natural forms of reasoning.

Indeed, if one takes one of the non-trivial axiomatic arithmetics containing all the truths of the standard model, there will be a formula of the language $Pr(x)$ which represents provability in the theory itself. It is then a simple matter to construct a sentence, G, in effect of the form $\neg Pr(\langle G \rangle)$ (where angle brackets indicate Gödel coding), and establish that both $\neg Pr(\langle G \rangle)$ and $Pr(\langle G \rangle)$ hold in the theory.[33]

What of Gödel's second theorem? Since a paraconsistent theory of the kind we have just been talking about is inconsistent, one should not expect to prove consistency. But it is also non-trivial, that is, some statements are not provable. This can be expressed by the sentence $\exists x \neg Pr(x)$, and this sentence can be proved in theories of the kind in question. Of course, this does not rule out the possibility that one may be able to prove $\neg \exists x \neg Pr(x)$ as well; and in what sense the proof of non-triviality is finitary may depend on other features of

---

[31] See Priest (2019b).

[32] See Priest (2006a), ch. 17.

[33] Additionally, one would expect that the schema $Pr(\langle A \rangle) \supset A$ would be provable in a theory of arithmetic in which $Pr(x)$ really did represent provability. In a consistent theory, it is not, as Löb's theorem shows. However, the schema is provable in the preceding theories.

the arithmetic. To what extent these matters may be thought to help Hilbert's program is, then, still a moot point.[34]

1.10 Intuitionist and Paraconsistent Mathematics

We have now been rather swiftly through a story of the development of studies in the foundations of mathematics in the last 150 years. As we have seen, none of the foundational ideas we have looked at can claim to have met with uncontestable success. But looking back over developments, we can see that something else has emerged.

As we saw in Section 1.6, there are fields of intuitionist mathematics that are quite different from their classical counterparts.[35] Indeed, there are fields of intuitionist mathematics that have no natural classical counterpart at all.

Let me give just one example of this. This is the Kock–Lawvere theory of smooth infinitesimal analysis.[36] To motivate this, consider how one would compute the derivative of a function, $f(x)$, using infinitesimals. The derivative, $f'(x)$, is the slope of the function at x, given an infinitesimal displacement, i; so $f(x + i) - f(x) = if'(x)$. Now, as an example, take $f(x)$ to be x^3. Then $if'(x) = (x + i)^3 - x^3 = 3x^2i + 3xi^2 + i^3$. If we could divide by i, we would have $3x^2 + 3xi + i^2$. Setting i to 0 delivers the result – though how, then, did we divide by i?[37] If $i^2 = 0$, we have another route to the answer. For then it follows that for any infinitesimal, i, $if'(x) = 3x^2i$. We may not be able to divide by i, but suppose that $ai = bi$, for all i, implies that $a = b$ (this is the *Principle of Microcancellation*). Then $f'(x) = 3x^2$ follows. This is exactly how the theory of smooth infinitesimal analysis proceeds.

Call a real number, i, a *nilsquare* if $i^2 = 0$. Of course, 0 itself is a nilsquare, but it may not be the only one! We may think of the nilsquares as infinitesimals. The theory of smooth infinitesimals takes functions to be linear on these. Given a function, f, there is a unique r such that, for every nilsquare, i, $f(x + i) - f(x) = ri$. (In effect, r is the derivative of f at x.) This is the *Principle of Microaffineness*.[38]

---

[34] A third foundational issue opened up by paraconsistency concerns category theory. Given that one can operate in a set theory with a universal set, it is possible to have a category of all sets, all groups, and so on, where 'all' means *all*. The implications of this for the relationship between set theory and category theory are yet to be investigated.

[35] For a further account of some of these enterprises, see Dummett (2000), chs. 2 and 3, and Posy (2020).

[36] On which, see Bell (2008).

[37] One answer to the conundrum is provided by non-standard analysis, an account of infinitesimals developed in the 1960s by Robinson. This deploys non-standard (classical) models of the theory of real numbers.

[38] Microcancellation follows. Take $f(x)$ to be xa. Then, taking x to be 0, Microaffineness implies that there is a unique r such that, for all i, $ai = ri$. So if $ai = bi$ for all i, $a = r = b$.

Microaffineness implies that 0 is not the only nilsquare. For suppose that it is; then all we have is that $f(x + 0) - f(x) = r0$, and clearly this does not define a unique r. So:

[1] $\neg \forall i(i^2 = 0 \rightarrow i = 0)$

But now, why do we need intuitionist logic? Well, one might argue that 0 *is* the only nilsquare, which would make a mess of things. A typical piece of reasoning for this goes as follows. Suppose that i is a nilsquare and that $\neg i = 0$. Then i has an inverse, i^{-1}, such that $i \cdot i^{-1} = 1$. But then $i^2 \cdot i^{-1} = i$. Since $i^2 = 0$, it follows that $i = 0$. Hence, by reductio, we have shown that $\neg \neg i = 0$. If we were allowed to apply Double Negation, we could infer that $i = 0$ – and so we would have a contradiction on our hands. But this move is not legitimate in intuitionist logic. We have just:

[2] $\forall i(i^2 = 0 \rightarrow \neg \neg i = 0)$.

And we may hold both [1] and [2] together.[39]

What we see, then, is that there are very distinctive fields of intuitionistic mathematics, quite different from the fields of classical mathematics. Moreover, one does not have to think that intuitionism is *philosophically* correct to recognise that these are interesting mathematical enterprises with their own integrity. They are perfectly good parts of pure mathematics. (Whether they have applications to areas outside of mathematics is a quite separate matter, and irrelevant.)

A similar point can be made with respect to paraconsistent mathematics. In Section 1.9 we saw that there were inconsistent mathematical theories relevant to various foundational enterprises: set theory and arithmetic. There are, however, many interesting inconsistent mathematical theories based on paraconsistent logics, which have no immediate application to foundational matters. These include theories in linear algebra, geometry, and topology.[40]

Let me give an example of one of these. This concerns boundaries. Take a simple topological space, say the Euclidean plane. Divide it into two disjoint parts, left, L, and right, R, divided by the line $x = 0$. Now consider a point,

---

[39] An example of a quite different kind: Some intuitionist theories of the reals contain both Brouwer's Continuity Theorem (every real-valued function defined over the closed unit interval [0,1] of a real variable is uniformly continuous on that interval) and Intuitionistic Church's Thesis (every total function from the natural numbers into the natural numbers is Turing computable). By suitable interpretations, one can understand each of these in classical terms; but not both together, by a construction of Specker. See Bridges and Richman (1987).

[40] See Mortensen (1995), Weber (2021), and (2022).

p, on this line. Is it in *L* or *R*? Of course, the description under-determines an answer to the question. But when the example is fleshed out, considerations of symmetry might suggest that it is in both. Then, $p \in L$, and $p \in R$ so $p \notin L -$ and symmetrically for *R*. So a description of the space might be that if $x \leq 0$, then $\langle x,y \rangle \in L$, and if $x \geq 0$, then $\langle x,y \rangle \in R$. Hence, if $x = 0$, $\langle x,y \rangle \in L \cap R$, even though $L \cap R = \emptyset$.[41]

This might not seem particularly interesting, but the idea of inconsistent boundaries has interesting applications. One of these is to describe the geometry of 'impossible pictures'.[42] Consider Figure 1.

Figure 1

The three-dimensional content of the picture is impossible. How should one describe it mathematically? Any mathematical characterisation will specify, amongst other things, the orientations of the various faces. Now, consider the left-hand face, and in particular its lighter shaded part. This is 90° to the horizontal. Next, consider the top of the lower step on the right-hand side of the picture. This is 0° to the horizontal. Finally, consider the boundary between them (a vertical line on the diagram). This is on both planes. Hence it is at both 90° and 0° to the horizontal.[43] That's a contradiction, since it cannot be both; but that's exactly what makes the content of the picture impossible. Note that the characterisation of the content must deploy a paraconsistent logic, since it should not imply, for example, that the top of the higher step is at 90° to the horizontal. Hence, we see, again, that whatever one thinks about the truth of naive set theory, or inconsistent arithmetic, there are perfectly good mathematical structures based on a paraconsistent logic.

Both intuitionist logic and paraconsistent logic, then, provide perfectly coherent and interesting areas of mathematical investigation to which classical logic can be applied only with disaster.[44]

---

[41] Further on inconsistent boundaries, see Cotnoir and Weber (2015).

[42] For more on the following, see Mortensen (2010).

[43] And one can set things up in such a way that this does not imply that 90 = 0.

[44] It seems to me that, given any formal logic, there could, at least in principle, be interesting mathematical theories based on this. However, I think it fair to say that intuitionistic logic and paraconsistent logic are the logics for which this has most clearly been shown.

1.11 Mathematical Pluralism Appears

What we have now seen is that there are distinct areas of relatively autonomous mathematical research. That is, there is a plurality of areas, such that there is no one of them to which all others can be reduced. In truth, this pluralism was already clear in the case of category theory: attempts to reduce it to set theory, or vice versa, were always straining at the seams. But intuitionist and paraconsistent mathematics have put the matter beyond doubt.

Establishing such a plurality was certainly not an aim of work in the foundations of mathematics, but it has emerged none the less. In the eighteenth century, some mathematicians investigated Euclidean geometry, trying to prove that the Parallel Postulate was deducible from the other axioms. They did this by assuming its negation, and aiming for a contradiction, which, it turned out, was not forthcoming. Their aim was not to produce non-Euclidean geometries; but by the nineteenth century, it became clear that this is exactly what they had done. In a similar way, the aim of research in the foundations of mathematics was not to establish the plurality of mathematics – indeed, most researchers in the area took themselves to be searching for a unique unifying foundation. But that, it seems, is what, collectively, they have done. If one were Hegel, one would surely diagnose here a fascinating episode in the cunning of reason.

1.12 Conclusion

In this section, we have seen how mathematical pluralism has arisen naturally out of research in the foundations of mathematics. Against this background, we can now look more closely at what mathematical pluralism is. We will turn to this matter in the next section.

2 An Examination of Mathematical Pluralism

2.1 Introduction

In the previous section I tracked the foundational project in the philosophy of mathematics – and its gradual disintegration, giving rise to mathematical pluralism. It is now time to look at mathematical pluralism itself more closely.[45]

---

[45] *Brief Review of Literature*: Mathematical pluralism is defended at length by Shapiro (2014). He argues for the position for much the same reason that I do. The plurality of mathematics is defended largely on the ground of constructive mathematics in Davies (2005). It is defended on the grounds of both constructive mathematics and category theory in Hellman and Bell (2006). A variety of mathematics, including classical and various constructive mathematics, is defended in Sambin (2011). Sambin does so, obtaining these mathematics in question by varying parameters within a 'minimalist foundation' of mathematics (distinct from set theory).

I explained mathematical pluralism in nuce in the preface. The first half of this section looks in more detail at the position and some of its central features. We will then turn to some objections to mathematical pluralism. What comes after this will require a prior discussion of Hamkins' view of the set-theoretic multiverse. That in place, we will then turn to another aspect of mathematical pluralism. This concerns relationships between structures; and that gives rise to another objection to pluralism (perhaps the most tricky). A discussion of this brings the section to a conclusion. In an appendix, I will make some brief remarks concerning the relevance of mathematical pluralism to the question of the ontological status of mathematical entities.

2.2 Mathematical Pluralism

The aim of mathematics – pure mathematics; we will get to applied mathematics in due course – is to formulate certain abstract structures and investigate them: number systems, algebras, topologies, geometries, categories, or wot not. A structure, here, is to be understood simply as a bunch of objects furnished with certain functions, properties, and relations, all governed by a particular logic.[46] These are, of course, described in a language; and in modern mathematics, this would normally be taken to be a formal language of some kind. Structures are characterised (that is, our grasp of them is provided) by a bunch of statements of the language. In modern mathematics, these would usually be given explicitly as axioms or rules. But such formalities played little role on mathematics outside of geometry till the late nineteenth century. So details may simply be implicit in a practice.

The foundational project was to formulate, investigate, and justify one over-arching system in which all other structures reside. To the extent that an orthodoxy on the subject still remains, this is the framework provided by Zermelo–Fraenkel set theory with the Axiom of Choice, *ZFC*. However, as we saw in the last section, even before the appearance of non-classical mathematics it was becoming clear that it was impossible to fit all mathematics into this

---

However, this framework hardly covers the whole variety of mathematics. Newton da Costa has long defended the legitimacy of paraconsistent mathematics as well as classical mathematics. (See, e.g., da Costa (1974).) Warren (2015) gives an argument for mathematical pluralism based on a conventionalism about meaning. A version of mathematical pluralism within his theory of objects is endorsed in Zalta (2023). And versions of mathematical pluralism *within* classical mathematics are defended by Balaguer (1995) and Clarke-Doane (2022), 3.5. A view she terms 'pluralism in mathematics' is described by Friend (2014). Despite having some elements in common with mathematical pluralism as I use that phrase, it is a very different view.

[46] To forestall any possible confusion, let me note that the fact that I use the word 'structure' does not imply that mathematical pluralism has anything to do with the philosophical view called 'structuralism'.

procrustean framework. This was made salient by category theory. But, in truth, studies in set theory also suggested this. Even leaving aside the set theories very different from *ZFC*, such as Quine's *NF* or Ackermann's set theory,[47] set theorists investigate systems of set theory which *extend ZFC*, such as those provided by the addition of large cardinal axioms.[48] They also investigate set theories which contain axioms inconsistent with *ZFC*, such as the Axiom of Determinacy or various axioms concerning non-well-founded sets.[49] Then they investigate distinctive but proper subsystems of *ZFC*, such as predicative set theory.[50] Clearly, we already have a plurality here.

These difficulties are all dwarfed by the problem for a hegemonic account posed by mathematical structures based on non-classical logics, again as we saw in the last section. These force one to go outside the framework, not just of *ZFC*, but of classical logic. What remains when one has done so is a vast plurality which resists being fitted into any uniform framework. That there is no such framework is the first substantial claim of mathematical pluralism. There is an irreducible plurality of mathematical structures, and mathematical truths are always secundum quid – that is, relative to a structure. So, properly understood, all mathematical truths are of the form *In structure* $\mathfrak{A}$, *A* – though the prefix may be taken for granted, and one may even be unaware that it is there.

The second major claim of mathematical pluralism is that all pure mathematical structures are, qua mathematical structure, equally good. There is no sense in which any of them is right and the others wrong. In the same way, there is no sense to the question of whether, as mathematical structures, Euclidean geometry is better than projective geometry, topology is better than recursion theory, set theory is better than category theory, or the intuitionist theory of smooth infinitesimals is better than the classical calculus. Of course, this does not mean that all structures are equal in other regards. Some may be more interesting, powerful, deep, rich, elegant, applicable, or whatever. That is another matter. Indeed some structures will fare very badly in these regards. Thus, take the structure with one object, *a*, one monadic property, *P*, such that *Pa* and ¬*Pa*, and whose underlying logic is the paraconsistent logic *LP*, so that everything in the language is true of *a* in the structure. This is a perfectly good mathematical structure – just a singularly boring one. And of course, there are singularly boring structures in classical mathematics as well, such as the 1-element group.

---

[47] See Holmes (2017).
[48] See Koellner (2010).
[49] See Koellner (2013) and Moss (2018), respectively.
[50] See Avron (2010) for discussion and references.

Naturally, one may ask what makes all of these structures *mathematics*, once one has given up the hegemony of *ZFC* and classical logic. I doubt that there is any essentialist answer to this question. The things which are mathematics are held together by strands of historical continuity – of the kind we tracked in the last section, but of course going back much, much, further. Nor is there any reason to suppose that the expanding list has come to an end. The list of new mathematical structures and their kinds will continue to expand – certainly for the foreseeable future, and maybe indefinitely. If one wants to say something about the relationship between the things on the list, perhaps the best one can do is to appeal to something like Wittgenstein's notion of family resemblance.[51]

2.3 Two Important Features of Mathematical Pluralism

Let us now note two particularly important points about mathematical pluralism. First, and most obviously, every structure in the plurality is based on some underlying logic or other, maybe classical, maybe intuitionist or paraconsistent, maybe something else. We may call this logic *the internal logic of the structure*, since what holds in the structure is closed under the consequence relation of that logic. The internal logic of a structure could be any logic. Thus, there are already well-established theories of a universe of sets based on many non-classical logics: set theory with the axioms of *ZFC*, but an underlying intuitionist logic; set theory based on the intuitionistic notion of a spread; fuzzy set theory based on, say, Łukasiewicz continuum-valued logic; set theory based on a relevant logic; set theory based on quantum logic.[52] The internal logic itself may be specified formally or, as the mathematics itself, simply be implicit in a practice.[53]

Next, one does not have to think that intuitionism or dialetheism (or whatever) is *philosophically* correct to subscribe to mathematical pluralism. One does not even have to hold that intuitionist or a paraconsistent logic is the one true logic (whatever one might take that to mean) to subscribe to mathematical pluralism. All one has to recognise is that the structures with these internal logics are all equally legitimate pure mathematical structures. Moreover, as we already saw in the last section, some of these have clear mathematical interest, even if one is as much a classical-logic monist as one

---

[51] Wittgenstein (1953), for example, §67.

[52] See, for example, Crosilla (2019), Van Atten (2017), §3, Hájek and Haniková (2003), Weber (2012), and Takeuti (1981), respectively.

[53] This raises the question as to what it is to follow the rules of a practice, as broached by Wittgenstein in the *Philosophical Investigations*; but that is far too large an issue to take on here. (For discussion, see Miller and Sultanescu (2022).) I suspect that, at some fundamental level, one has to say 'This is simply what I do' (Wittgenstein (1953), Remark 217).

can be. Of course, this does not imply that such a monist will be interested in such structures. Interest is a subjective matter, and most mathematicians are interested in only a few kinds of mathematical structures. Set theorists tend to have little interest in probability theory; geometers tend to have little interest in recursion theory; and so on.

2.4 Games and Other Practices

The investigation of a mathematical structure is, in an obvious sense, a rule-governed activity. Namely, to infer things that hold in the structure, one infers according to its internal logic. One pursues the pertinent inferential practice. Now, there are other rule-governed practices where there is clearly a pluralism of a kind similar to mathematical pluralism, namely games. Moreover, considering the similarities is a good way of bringing out some of the other features of mathematical pluralism. I stress that the analogy with games is just that: an analogy. And it should not be pushed too far, since there are clearly disanalogies too.[54] Perhaps most importantly, mathematics is a species of truth-seeking activity. Playing a game is not (at least, not in the same sense: you might have to establish the truth of some things in the course of playing a game). A consequence of this is that some parts of mathematics have applications. Games do not have applications in the same sense.

So let us consider some obvious facts about games:

1. There are many games; and any individual can play lots of different games. Thus, chess and go are such games.
2. One of these might be more interesting than another, more aesthetically pleasing, or have a richer structure. But, qua game, all are equally legitimate.
3. Games have rules. The rules may have been made explicit, as in the case of chess and go; or they may only be implicit in a practice, as are many children's games (or as are the grammatical rules of a language).
4. The rules may be learned explicitly – as, normally, one learns chess; or they may simply be picked up by entering into the game and having one's actions corrected until, in the end, one just 'has a feel' for what to do.
5. Whichever of these is the case, playing the game is just following the rules.
6. Typically, there is a point to following the rules: winning – which is not to say that a person must have the personal aim of winning to play the game; just that it's the institutional point.[55]

---

[54] Though I push the analogy a little further in Priest (2013a).

[55] Of course, in some things we are inclined to call games there are no winners or losers. These, presumably, have other points.

Bearing these things in mind, let us consider the similarities with mathematical pluralism. There is a plurality of mathematical investigatory practices: concerning category theory, intuitionist analysis, inconsistent calculus, and so on. Each of these is governed by a set of rules of inference, and engaging in the practice means following those rules. The (institutional) point of following the rules is establishing (proving) certain things that hold in the structures concerned. The rules may be explicit, as they typically are in contemporary mathematics; or implicit, as they were with number theory until the late nineteenth century. One may absorb the rules simply by being trained to follow them, as one learns a first language; arithmetic is usually learned in this way. Or one may learn the rules more reflectively, as one learns a second language; the way that a classically trained mathematician has to struggle with intuitionistic proof when they first meet intuitionist mathematics is like this. And just as with games, some practices may be more interesting, fruitful, or whatever; but all the practices, qua practices, are equally legitimate.[56]

There is also a strong similarity between the phenomenology of playing certain games and of mathematical investigations. When one learns certain games – take chess as an example – one is initially very conscious of the rules. ('This is a knight; now, how does it move?') Once one internalises the rules, one no longer thinks of them, however. They create a phenomenologically objective space, within which one just moves around. Similarly, when one learns a new mathematical practice, one has to concentrate very hard on the rules. ('This is a group; now, what properties does the group operator have?', 'We are doing intuitionistic mathematics; now, is this a legitimate inferential move?') But once the rules are internalised, the phenomenology changes, and we again find ourselves within an objective terrain within which we move around.

2.5 Some Objections

Let us now consider some natural objections to mathematical pluralism.

Objection 1. There is no real plurality here, since all the mathematics fit into a single framework. Of course, the framework cannot be *ZFC*, for reasons that I have already discussed, but there is some other framework.

Perhaps the production of some kind of *ur*-mathematics to which all the kinds of mathematics we have met can be reduced, might be thought of as some kind of foundational project for the twenty-first century. But the variety of mathematics would appear to make the realisation of such a project some

---

[56] And of course, just as new games can be designed (with trials concerning the best rules), so can new mathematical practices.

kind of pipe dream. Clearly, there is nothing even remotely like this on the horizon.

One might contest this. All the mathematics can be accommodated in classical model theory. Structures are simply set-theoretic models, in the sense of model theory. And our *ur*-mathematics is simply the investigation of such models in, say, *ZFC* – even if the internal logics of the models may be non-classical.

This suggestion fails. First, it is not at all clear that structures are set-theoretic models. The 'standard interpretation' of Peano Arithmetic is a structure (the 'natural numbers'). But asking which set the number 3 is has no clear sense. Of course, there are set theoretic structures which, under appropriate assumptions, are isomorphic to this structure. The trouble is, there are lots. This has been a very familiar problem in the philosophy of mathematics since Benacerraf's classic 'What Numbers could not Be'.[57] And to go into the vast literature the paper has spawned would take us away from the main issue here.[58] So I just note the point, and move on.

Even setting this issue aside, there appear to be insuperable problems in implementing the details of the suggestion. Most obviously, there seems to be no way to pursue this strategy in the case of category theory, simply because the foundational problem with category theory was precisely that its ambit appears to outstrip the classical models. Category theory has long been recognised as not fitting into *ZFC* in any non-gerrymandered way, as I discussed in the last section.[59]

Next, if we have a non-classical theory, it may indeed have models which can be formulated in *ZFC*. And examining the models may well tell you something about the theory – perhaps most notably, what cannot be proved. But examining a theory and examining its models are not the same thing – even when both are formulated in classical logic. Investigating what can be proved about numbers on the basis of Peano Arithmetic is quite a different enterprise from investigating the structure of the collection of its models, standard and non-standard.

Finally, the insistence that the model theory must be classical is, from a pluralist perspective, simply dogmatic. Investigations could proceed, for example, with intuitionist model theory, which would give quite different results.[60]

[57] Benacerraf (1965).

[58] See, further, Reck and Schiemer (2019).

[59] See, also, for example, Engeler and Röhrl (1969).

[60] Intuitionist model theory is well established; a general paraconsistent model theory is still a work in progress.

Objection 2: There may be a plurality of pure mathematical structures, but some of them are privileged in an important way.

Now, whether all the members of the plurality are equally deep, elegant, applicable, or whatever, as the favoured mathematics, might certainly be an issue. But, as noted, that is beside the point. Moreover, saying that non-classical mathematical structures are not really mathematics strikes me as the equivalent of the proverbial ostrich burying its head in the sand: these theories have clear mathematical interest. Indeed, such topics appear in (rigorously refereed) mainstream mathematics journals and in books with well-established publishing houses.[61]

One might try pointing to a different form of privilege. To illustrate it, take, for example, Peano Arithmetic, PA. $PA + Con(PA)$ is 'legitimate', that is, true; and $PA + \neg Con(PA)$ is not.[62] The argument appeals to a notion of truth simpliciter, whereas pluralism holds that all truth is secundum quid. $PA + Con(PA)$ is true in the structure which is the standard model (we hope!); $PA + \neg Con(PA)$ is not, but is true in some other structures. So the argument begs the question. If, as it is standard to assume, syntactic structures, such as formulas and proofs, may be coded up by numbers, this shows that such notions are also relative to particular structures – much as logicians may be habituated to thinking otherwise.

It may be retorted that since Peano Arithmetic *is* consistent, and $Con(PA)$ expresses this fact, it *is* true simpliciter. But $Con(PA)$ is a purely number-theoretic statement. If it has any other sense – say, concerning what humans or (physical) computational devices can or cannot do – this is a matter of applied mathematics, not of pure mathematics.[63]

Of course, mathematicians – or at least philosophers of mathematics – are not used to thinking of things in this way. They do not normally think it necessary to prefix 'true' with 'in the standard model' when making claims about arithmetic. Three hundred years ago, mathematicians did not think it necessary to prefix 'true' with 'in Euclidean geometry' when making claims about geometry. We now know that one needs to do so. True again, we have not been aware of different theories of arithmetic till relatively recently. This may explain the blind spot, but it does not justify it.

---

[61] What makes something of mathematical interest? I doubt that there is a precise answer to this question. Perhaps one cannot do much better than what was done by Justice Potter in *Jacobellis* v. *Ohio* (1964) when he said of pornography something to the effect of the following: I cannot define it, but I know it when I see it.

[62] The objection comes from Koellner (2009). See esp. the end of §§1.3 and 3.

[63] See Section 3. See also Warren (2015).

Likely at this point, some appeal will be made to the fact that the standard model of arithmetic is distinctive in that it correctly encodes our ordinary counting practices. Perhaps it does; perhaps it does not. But this gives the standard model no privileged pure mathematical status. As pure mathematics, all practices are equal. Moreover, this just confuses pure mathematics with applied mathematics. It is equally the case that Euclidean geometry correctly encoded our spatial measuring practices (at least until recently). That does not even show that such a practice is correct for that application, let alone that it cannot be revised if appropriate empirical circumstances arise. I will take up the matter of applied mathematics in the next section.

Objection 3: *This is just a version of formalism.* Mathematical pluralism is just a version of the view that mathematics is simply the development of formal systems; that is, mathematics is nothing more than symbol-manipulation in each such system.[64] This view is sometimes described by saying that mathematics is a game with symbols.[65]

Now, whilst there are certainly some similarities between this version of formalism and the view that I am suggesting here, there are crucial differences. For a start, there is no suggestion that an arbitrary formal system is a mathematical one: the system must have mathematical content of some kind. Nor is there a suggestion that every mathematical investigation is a formal system. People were 'playing the game' of arithmetic for millennia before it was formalised. Perhaps it cannot even be formalised. (If it is essentially a second-order theory, it cannot.)

Next, mathematical pluralism is naturally understood as a view according to which mathematics is *about* the things the mathematical terms refer to. (I defer a brief discussion of this point to the appendix of this section.) This is explicitly denied by formalists.

Finally, and to return to matters phenomenological, the phenomenologies of doing mathematics and of manipulating symbols are quite different, as I have just stressed. When one learns a branch of mathematics initially, one may be doing little more than operating on symbols according to rules; but the phenomenology of a fully fledged mathematical practice is exactly one of acquaintance with the objects that the symbols (noun phrases) refer to.

Objection 4. The view makes nonsense of certain debates in the foundations of mathematics. For example, Brouwer and similar intuitionists famously held that classical mathematicians had got it wrong; and paraconsistent set-theorists

---

[64] Something like this view is to be found in Curry (1951). For a discussion of the various forms of formalism and their problems, see Weir (2019).
[65] See Horsten (2017), §3.

have argued that *ZFC* gets our set theory wrong. If all these structures are equally legitimate, these debates have no substance, contrary to appearances

No. It is true that the debates, conceived of as ones as to which theory is correct are simply mistaken. (And it is not the first time in philosophy that philosophical debates have turned out to be based on false assumptions, and so entirely mistaken.) However, the debates can be understood in another and substantial way.

In each case there is or was a received practice, number theoretic reasoning, set theoretic reasoning, or whatever. But there can be legitimate disputes about what, exactly, the correct norms of that practice are. We formulate different sets of rules, trying to capture these. There can be a fact of the matter about who, if anyone, gets it right. In the same way, linguists can take a spoken language and try to formulate a set of rules which capture its grammar. Some grammars can just be wrong. Of course, once a set of formal rules is set up, they do characterise some language or other; and even if it is not the one targeted, it can likely still be used. Similarly, once rules for a mathematical practice are explicitly formulated, they can be followed. Thus, an advocate of paraconsistent set theory with unlimited comprehension does not have to claim that *ZFC* is wrong. *ZFC* is just as good a practice (qua practice) as paraconsistent set theory. It is just that those who adhere to it are wrong if they claim that it correctly characterises our naive theory of sets.

2.6 Interlude: Hamkins' Multiverse

There is one further important aspect of mathematical pluralism that needs to be discussed. However, for reasons that will become clear in due course, let me say a few words about Hamkins' multiverse view of set theory first.[66]

A standard view of sets is that there is a unique structure which is the totality of all sets. This is the cumulative hierarchy, $\mathbb{V}$. *ZFC* describes the structure – at least partially: there are important properties of sets that cannot be settled by the axioms of *ZFC* – notoriously the Continuum Hypothesis, *CH*. This incompleteness has led to a search for additional axioms, notably large cardinal axioms, which can settle the matter. The search has been strikingly unsuccessful. On the other hand, set theoretic techniques such as forcing have shown us how to construct models of *ZFC* in which *CH* holds and models in which ¬*CH* holds.

Hamkins' response to this situation is to suggest that one should think of *ZFC*, not as like Peano Arithmetic, with an intended interpretation, but as

---

[66] See, for example, Hamkins (2012) and (2020), ch. 8.

like group theory, with multiple realisations. And just as some groups are commutative and some are not, some realisations of *ZFC* are *CH*-verifying, and some are not.

Now, a mathematical pluralist is not obliged to accept Hamkins' view of set theory. For all we have seen so far, there could be an intended interpretation of *ZFC*. But, clearly, pluralism accommodates the view naturally: there is a plurality of structures that realise the axioms of *ZFC*, and they are all equally legitimate. Moreover, given the apparently tenuous nature of our grip on a determinate standard interpretation of *ZFC*, the view is a very enticing one. Our grasp of any structure would appear to be given by its characterisation. But the determination of the *CH* (etc.) appears to go beyond any characterisation we possess. Therefore there cannot be a unique such structure.

Naturally, the mathematical pluralist will go Hamkins one better. There is nothing sacrosanct about *ZFC* and classical logic. As we have already noted, there is a genuine plurality of set theories based on different logics, and the thought that these are all incomplete versions of an intended interpretation would just be bizarre. In fact, Hamkins is alive to this possibility:[67]

> The background idea of the multiverse, of course, is that there should be a large collection of universes, each a model of (some kind of) set theory. There seems to be no reason to restrict inclusion only to *ZFC* models, as we can include models of weaker theories *ZF*, *KP⁻*, *KP*, and so on, perhaps even down to second-order number theory, as this is set-theoretic in a sense.

No mention here of theories with underlying non-classical logics; but given pluralism, this is a natural extrapolation.

2.7 Higher-Order Structures

Now let us turn to a highly important feature of mathematical pluralism. Give a mathematician a structure, $\mathfrak{A}$, the first thing they will want to do is to see what holds in the structure. They will do so by proving things which follow from its characterisation using its internal logic.

The second thing they will want to do is prove things *about* the structure; that is, they will want to determine the properties of the structure itself; doubtless they will also want to show how it relates to other structures, that is, to establish relations between it and other structures.[68] Clearly this requires $\mathfrak{A}$ to be an object in the domain of a 'higher-order' structure, $\mathfrak{B}$ (though if $\mathfrak{A}$ is

---

[67] Hamkins (2012), p. 436.
[68] As noted, for example, by Shapiro (2014), p. 171.

non-well-founded in an appropriate sense, $\mathfrak{B}$ could be $\mathfrak{A}$ itself).[69] Standardly, $\mathfrak{B}$ will be a set theoretic or category theoretic structure, and one would think of $\mathfrak{B}$ as providing a metatheory for $\mathfrak{A}$. But $\mathfrak{A}$ can naturally be seen as an object in many such structures. Which one should be used for the second project? The answer a pluralist should give is obvious. Just as there is no privileged 'object-level' structure, there is no privileged 'meta-level' structure. Hamkins has again been here before us:[70]

> The multiverse perspective ultimately provides what I view as an enlargement of the theory/metatheory distinction. There are not merely two sides for this distinction, the object theory and the metatheory, but rather there is a vast hierarchy of metatheories. Every set-theoretic context, after all, provides in effect a meta-theoretic background for the models and theories that exist in that context, a model theory for the models and theories one finds there. Every model of set theory provides an interpretation of second-order logic, for example, using the sets and predicates existing there. Yet, a given model of set theory M may itself be a model inside a larger model of set theory N, and so what was previously the absolute set-theoretic background, for the people living inside M, becomes just one of the possible models of set theory, from the perspective of the larger model N. Each meta-theoretic context becomes just another model at the higher level. In this way, we have theory, metatheory, metametatheory and so on, a vast hierarchy of possible set-theoretic backgrounds.

Hamkins does not say so explicitly, but given that all the members of the multiverse are equally kosher, so are all the different metatheories.

Notice the implications of this view. If $\mathfrak{A}$ lives in (that is, is one of the objects in) $\mathfrak{B}_1$ and $\mathfrak{B}_2$, then it may have different properties in these two superstructures. For example, it may be countable in $\mathfrak{B}_1$ and uncountable in $\mathfrak{B}_2$.[71] Note, moreover, that there is no reason why $\mathfrak{A}$ and a $\mathfrak{B}$ in which it lives must have the same internal logic. Thus, a classical structure (one whose truths are closed under classical logic) may be an object in a paraconsistent structure. (Classical structures can be thought of as special cases of paraconsistent structures – ones where truth and falsity in the structure do not overlap.)[72]

---

[69] Note that such an embedding may even be deployed for 'first-order' purposes. Thus the Wiles proof of Fermat's Last Theorem (about natural numbers) goes via an embedding of the natural numbers into a larger structure: the complex numbers. See, further, Priest (2013a), sect. 4.

[70] Hamkins (2020), p. 298.

[71] A striking example of this is given by Hamkins and Yang (2013). They argue that, where $\mathfrak{A}$ is a model of arithmetic, there can be two models of ZFC, $\mathfrak{B}_1$ and $\mathfrak{B}_2$, and sentences, A, of first-order arithmetic, such that in $\mathfrak{B}_1$, $\mathfrak{A} \models A$ and in $\mathfrak{B}_2$, $\mathfrak{A} \models \neg A$. This is essentially because the definition of $\models$ is second-order, and $\mathfrak{B}_1$ and $\mathfrak{B}_2$ have different power sets of the natural numbers.

[72] Thus, for example, let $\mathfrak{A}$ be a classical (and a fortiori an LP) model of ZFC. $\omega \in V_{\omega+1}$. Now using the collapsing lemma (Priest (2006a), 18.4) one can construct the model, $\mathfrak{A}'$, of ZFC,

Or an intuitionistic structure (one whose truths are closed only under intuitionist logic) may occur in a classical universe. For example, Kripke models for intuitionistic logic may well be (and often are) formulated within a classical metatheory (such as *ZFC*).

Moreover, if $\mathfrak{B}_1$ and $\mathfrak{B}_2$ have different internal logics, they might well establish strikingly different things about $\mathfrak{A}$. For example, Kripke models for intuitionist logic are complete, given a classical metalanguage; but not, given an intuitionist metalanguage.[73] Different superstructures are, then, liable to deliver quite different perspectives on $\mathfrak{A}$, so to speak. And given mathematical pluralism, all are equally correct. Of course, if one does not wish to be confused, one needs to be clear which superstructure one is working in – just as, if one is playing a game, one had better be clear about what that game is – or one may suffer the mathematical analogue of picking up the ball and running with it whilst playing soccer.

In his book on logical and mathematical pluralism, Shapiro sums up his discussion of a closely related point as follows:[74]

> To conclude and to repeat, in order to do any deductive reasoning, especially in highly mathematized areas like logic, meta-logic, semantics, and meta-semantics, one must invoke a logic. In certain intellectual climates, it might be a good idea, or just plain courteous, to explicitly acknowledge which logic one is using. However, on the present, eclectic orientation to logic, nothing prevents a theorist committed to a substantial logic from studying a range of other logics and learning how they relate to each other and her own. Nor does it prevent another logician from taking on a similar study; using a different logic. Nor does it prevent a third logician from studying how the first two meta-theoretic projects relate to each other. The three of them may not be able to share all of their results with each other, in a straightforward homophonic manner, but that's life.

Indeed it is.[75]

---

which identifies all the members of $V_{\omega+2}$ into a single object, x. Then in $\mathfrak{A}'$, ω is a consistent structure, in the sense that the membership relation restricted to ω is consistent; but $\omega \in x$ and $\omega \notin x$.

[73] See McCarty (1991). For further discussion of this sort of variability, see Shapiro (2014), ch. 7.

[74] Shapiro (2014), p. 204.

[75] One might well ask: what is it that makes $\mathfrak{A}$ the same object in higher-order structures $\mathfrak{B}_1$ and $\mathfrak{B}_2$? I suppose that one might deny that this is ever the case. This would seem too extreme a view, however. If $\mathfrak{A}$, $\mathfrak{B}_1$, and $\mathfrak{B}_2$ are set theoretic structures, and $\mathfrak{A}$ has the same members in $\mathfrak{B}_1$ and $\mathfrak{B}_2$, then it is the same set. This is a special case, however: some of the structures at issue may not be set-theoretic. (Maybe they are categories.) A general answer to the question raises a number of delicate issues – concerning, for example, meaning and reference. (For some discussion, see Shapiro (2014), ch. 5.) Fortunately, we do not need to go into the matter here.

2.8 Relativism and Regress

In the light of this, let us turn to a final objection to mathematical pluralism. It might be suggested that 'pluralism in metatheory' delivers a pernicious relativism.

Now, there is certainly a relativism here. The truth of a mathematical claim is relative to the structure employed. Or better: determinate mathematical claims must be taken to be of the form 'In structure $\mathfrak{A}$: A' – though often the prefix may be taken for granted. There is nothing pernicious about relativism of this kind. Many claims have a determinate truth value only with respect to a context, e.g. 'It is 18.00h'. (At what time zone?) Structures just deliver contexts of a certain kind.[76]

The fact that structures may live within structures raises an extra spectre here, though. If we say 'In structure $\mathfrak{A}$: A', that itself is a mathematical claim. In what structure is that supposed to hold? Clearly, an infinite regress threatens. And the worry is that all determinate truth is lost. A is not true, but only 'In $\mathfrak{A}_0$: A'; but that is not true, only 'In $\mathfrak{A}_1$: in $\mathfrak{A}_0$: A'; but that is not true, only 'In $\mathfrak{A}_2$: in $\mathfrak{A}_1$: in $\mathfrak{A}_0$: A'. And so on. All truth disappears in the process.

In fact, the regress may not go 'all the way up', but may ground out in a maximal structure of some kind – a structure which contains all structures of the kind in question. Thus, for example, the regress of set-theoretic structures may ground out in the cumulative hierarchy, the 'intended interpretation' of the axioms of *ZFC*. This, of course, assumes that it makes sense to talk of *the* cumulative hierarchy. One may claim that there is no such structure; either, as in Hamkins' view, because there is a multiverse, or because the universe is 'indefinitely extensible'.[77] But in any case, there are set theories, such as a naive set theory obtained by using a paraconsistent logic, which have a universal set. This contains every structure in the set theory, including itself. Of course, given mathematical pluralism one should not expect such maximal structures to be unique. There may be many of them (for example, using different underlying logics). So relativism is still with us, but the maximal structures ground out the regress threatened by the fact that structures may inhabit other structures.

But in any case, the regress is not vicious because of a subtle distinction which is easily overlooked. I don't think that there is a canonical name for it,

---

The issue of this section arises only if and when $\mathfrak{A}$ *does* preserve its identity across higher-order structures.

[76] A discussion and defence of a more general kind of mathematical relativism, sympathetic to mathematical pluralism, can be found in Bueno (2011). Note that mathematical pluralism itself is not a claim relative to anything. It is a claim of philosophy, not of mathematics, as Shapiro (2014), p. 183, notes.

[77] See Priest (2013b).

but let me call it that between what is true *within* a structure and what is true *about* a structure.

For analogy, consider fiction. Let me abbreviate *The Hound of the Baskervilles* as *HOB*. Consider the sentence:

- A detective called 'Sherlock Holmes' lives in Baker St.

This is actually false: no such detective ever lived in Baker St. But consider:

- In *HOB*: a detective called 'Sherlock Holmes' lives in Baker St.

This is a truth *about* a detective named 'Sherlock Holmes', but *within HOB*.

But now suppose that I write a story about me reading *HOB*. Suppose the story is called *Graham Priest Finds a Book* (*GPFB*). Graham Priest finds *HOB* in an old bookshop. He reports the contents of the book to a friend as follows:

- In *HOB* there is a detective called 'Sherlock Holmes', and he lives in Regent St.

What is said by me in the fiction is actually false. What *is* true is that:

- In *GPFB*: in *HOB*: there is a detective called 'Sherlock Holmes', and he lives in Regent St.

This is true *about HOB* and *within GPFB*. And – note – the story can be just as much about *HOB* as it is about me, even though what is said of both is false.[78]

Now, concerning structures, suppose I say:

- −1 has a square root.

This has no determinate truth value. All mathematical truth is secundum quid. The quid needs to be explicit (or at least taken for granted in the context). However, if $\mathfrak{R}$ and $\mathfrak{C}$ are the structures which are the real and complex numbers, respectively:

- In $\mathfrak{R}$: −1 has a square root.
- In $\mathfrak{C}$:−1 has a square root.

do have determinate truth values: the first is false; the second is true. These are statements *about* −1, but *within* $\mathfrak{R}$ and $\mathfrak{C}$.

---

[78] See Priest (2005), 2nd edn, 12.4.

The structures $\mathfrak{R}$ and $\mathfrak{C}$ are not themselves objects in $\mathfrak{R}$ and $\mathfrak{C}$, but they can be objects within a higher-order structure, say the cumulative hierarchy, $\mathfrak{V}$. So in *ZFC* one may say things like:

- In $\mathfrak{V}$: in $\mathfrak{C}$: -1 has a square root.

This is a truth *about* $\mathfrak{C}$, but *within* $\mathfrak{V}$.

Thus, a mathematical statement, A, may have no determinate truth value in itself, but it can have a determinate truth value *within* a structure. That structure can itself be an element of a higher-order structure. One can then make statements *about* that structure *within* the higher-order structure. In both cases, the structure within which one is operating may not be mentioned explicitly, but may be taken for granted.[79]

Now, the regress with which we started fails, since it trades on an ambiguity. The statement 'In $\mathfrak{A}_0$: A' can have a perfectly determinate truth value as a statement *within* $\mathfrak{A}_0$. But it can be a statement without a truth value, construed as a statement about $\mathfrak{A}_0$ within some (unspecified) higher-order structure – or more likely in practice, a statement with a determinate truth value within such a structure, which one being taken for granted. And of course, it can have different truth values with respect to two different such structures.

Indeed, what makes it easy to overlook the distinction I have been drawing is precisely the fact that, more often than not, the structure within which one is working is obvious and not mentioned. The game one is playing – so to speak – is taken for granted.

In Section 2.7 I said that, for the purpose of investigating the properties of a structure, $\mathfrak{A}$, any structure, $\mathfrak{B}$, in which $\mathfrak{A}$ is an object is equally good. It might be suggested that the preceding discussion shows that this claim should be qualified: a $\mathfrak{B}$ which 'gets things right' should be preferred. Specifically, call $\mathfrak{B}$ *faithful* to $\mathfrak{A}$ if for all A in the relevant language:

- (in $\mathfrak{B}$: in $\mathfrak{A}$: A) if and only if (in $\mathfrak{A}$: A)

where the left-hand side is within $\mathfrak{B}$ and the right-hand side is within $\mathfrak{A}$. Then for the purposes of investigating the properties of $\mathfrak{A}$, a faithful $\mathfrak{B}$ should be used.

Tempting as this thought is, it should be resisted. To see why, consider again the multiverse. Take a structure, $\mathfrak{A}$, which is a model of *ZFC*. Consider some set, x, in it, which it takes to be uncountable. It may be the case that there is

---

[79] If 'In $\mathfrak{A}$: A' is *within* $\mathfrak{A}$, one might think of 'In $\mathfrak{A}$' as a unitary prefix; whilst if it is *about* $\mathfrak{A}$, one might think of '$\mathfrak{A}$' as occupying a quantifiable position.

a structure, $\mathfrak{B}$, in which $\mathfrak{A}$ lives, according to which x is countable. Here, one may be inclined to say that $\mathfrak{B}$'s perspective on x is *more* accurate than that of $\mathfrak{A}$ itself, except that $\mathfrak{A}$ may live in another structure, $\mathfrak{C}$, in which x is still uncountable. Even worse: it can be the case that $\mathfrak{B}$, and so $\mathfrak{A}$, and so x, lives into some structure, $\mathfrak{D}$, according to which x is again uncountable.[80] There is simply no sense to the question of which perspective on matters is absolutely right.

2.9 Conclusion

In this section, we have looked at mathematical pluralism itself, what it is, some of its features, and some things that might be thought to cause problems for the view. I have argued that they do not.

So much for pure mathematics. But what, on this view of pure mathematics, is one to say about applied mathematics? We will turn to this in the next section.

2.10 Appendix: The Nature of Mathematical Objects

In Objection 3 of Section 2.5 I noted that a mathematical pluralist can happily hold that their formal investigations concern the mathematical objects which their formalism describes. Indeed, the view is almost mandatory, since the phenomenology of these investigations overwhelmingly appears to present such objects. The question then arises as to their ontological status. Several answers to the question are possible.

One may simply be a Platonist about the objects. Mathematical names, such as '3', refer to existent objects, and '3 is prime' is true since the object referred to has the property of primeness. Mathematical quantifiers range over a domain of such objects.

Mathematical pluralism puts certain demands on this picture, however. For a start, it must hold not just of the standard mathematical objects on which traditional mathematical platonism is fixated, such as numbers and the sets of *ZFC*, but of all objects and structures of the plurality of mathematics. One version of this view, advocated by Mark Balaguer and others, has come to be known as *Full Blooded Platonism* or *Plenitudinous Platonism*.[81] According to his view, every classically consistent specification characterises a structure, or family of structures, and all of these and their denizens are equally existent.[82]

---

[80] See Hamkins (2023).
[81] See Balaguer (1995).
[82] This is, in fact, a version of Hilbert's view that existence in mathematics is just consistency. See Doherty (2017).

The view needs to be handled with a certain amount of care, however, since mathematical objects can have contradictory properties in different structures. Thus, if *PA* is Peano Arithmetic, there will be structures that realise *PA* + *Con(PA)* and ones that realise *PA* + ¬*Con(PA)*. One would not want, on account of this fact, to say that *Con(PA)* and ¬*Con(PA)* are both true. One might attempt to solve this problem by saying that truth is a matter of what holds in the *intended* interpretation – or all the intended interpretations, if there is more than one. What one should make of the notion of an intended interpretation in general, is not entirely clear. However, given mathematical pluralism, there is a simple answer. All truth is secundum quid – relative to a structure; so, in the present case, in structure $\mathfrak{A}_1$, *Con(PA)* and in structure $\mathfrak{A}_2$, ¬*Con(PA)*. Neither *Con(PA)* nor ¬*Con(PA)* is true simpliciter.[83]

There is a bigger worry about this view, however.[84] Why restrict oneself to classically *consistent* structures? There is no reason for a mathematical pluralist to do this, since structures based on *other* logics may be consistent. And, once paraconsistent logic is brought into the picture, structures can, in any case, no longer be restricted to consistent ones. As we have seen, there are theories with clear mathematical interest which are inconsistent. Mathematical pluralism therefore requires the view to encompass *all* structures, consistent or otherwise – Beall calls this version of the view *Really Full Blooded Platonism*, or *Paraconsistent Plenitudinous Platonism*. Of course, this will now include very inconsistent structures, such as the one-point trivial structure, as I have already observed (Section 2.2). But no one said that existent structures have to be mathematically interesting. Some of the flowers in the garden may be much more beautiful and interesting than others; and some may be downright dull and boring. If one is going to be a platonist, then, this is the kind of platonism that mathematical pluralism requires.

Another possible view – and my own preferred position[85] – indeed, one suggested by phenomenological considerations, is the same as this, except that the objects and structures in question are non-existent objects (in which case, all the quantifiers used in the theory of the structure must be interpreted as 'existentially unloaded'). This is noneism.[86]

---

[83] I take it that this is, in fact, Balaguer's preferred solution. See Balaguer (1995), §4.

[84] As pointed out by Beall (1999).

[85] See Priest (2005), ch. 7.

[86] The view is often called 'Meinongianism', but the name is a poor one. For a start, the view that some objects do not exist was held by virtually every logician till the twentieth century – and by many important philosophers, such as Reid and Husserl. (See Priest (2005), 2nd ed., ch 18.) Moreover, Meinong held that abstract objects exist (*bestehen*), just not in space and time. Note that he did not hold that objects *bestehen* if they do not exist. This was Russell's view at one time, not his. (See Reicher (2019a), §4.)

Likely, it will be said that such a view makes no sense, since to be an object *just is* to be an existent object. This is surely false. I am sorry I may have to tell some readers that Sherlock Holmes does not exist. The stories are fictions, not histories. But if you are thinking about Sherlock Holmes, you are thinking about something (some thing). And (the Christian) God is certainly an object (e.g., of worship), but it is highly significant when an erstwhile Christian comes to the view that God does not exist – or vice versa for an erstwhile atheist.

Moreover, once one has taken this point to heart, there seems to be no particularly good reason – even when one takes the application of mathematics into account – to suppose that mathematical objects are *existent* objects. On the contrary: the fact that they have no causal effect on anything makes them pretty good candidates for non-existence.

In this context, I note that a version of mathematical pluralism is defended by Zalta (2023). His preferred ontology is that of Platonism, but as he has often stressed, one may reinterpret his system. If one takes the quantifiers not to be existentially loaded, and reads his predicate $E!$ as 'exists', we have a noneist account. The major difference between Zalta's mathematical pluralism and mine (as opposed to his account of noneism and mine[87]) is that he distinguishes between what he calls *natural mathematics* and *theoretical mathematics*. Theoretical mathematical claims are secundum quid, to be considered as prefixed by an operator of the form 'In theory T'. This is not exactly the same as my 'In structure $\mathfrak{A}$' but it plays a very similar role in this context. By contrast, natural mathematical claims are *true simpliciter*. Natural mathematical claims occur when we say things like 'the number of planets is eight' or 'the class of insects is larger than the class of humans'.[88] For me, such things are no concern of pure mathematics. How to understand them is a matter of applied mathematics, as we shall see in the next section.

A third way in which one may approach the question of the nature of mathematical objects, compatible with mathematical pluralism, is fictionalism. The label 'fictionalism' covers a fairly wide variety of views, even in the philosophy of mathematics,[89] but let us take Field's version of it.[90]

According to this view, terms like '3' do not refer to objects – existent or non-existent. They fail to refer at all. What exactly, then, to say about the status of statements such as '2 + 3 = 5' will depend on how one handles

---

[87] On the various kinds of noneism, see Reicher (2010b).

[88] Zalta (2023), p. 5.

[89] For fictionalism in general, see Eklund (2019); in the philosophy of mathematics in particular, see Balaguer (2018).

[90] See Field (1989), pp. 1–30.

sentences containing names which do not refer. But whatever one does here, such a sentence will not be true. Clearly, however, there is some sense in which this statement needs to be distinguished from the statement that '$2 + 3 = 47$'.

Field's answer is as follows. The sentence 'a famous detective lives in 221B Baker St' is false. What is true is that 'According to the Conan Doyle fictions a famous detective lives in 221B Baker St'. In the same way, '$2 + 3 = 5$' is not true. What is true is that, according to the standard 'mathematical fiction', $2+3 = 5$.[91] It is not true that according to this $2+3 = 47$, just as it is not true that according to the Conan Doyle fictions a famous nuclear physicist lives in 221B Baker St. Of course, if one is a mathematical pluralist, standard mathematics has no privileged status. Any mathematical characterisation, whether explicit in an axiomatisation, or implicit in a practice, will deliver a legitimate 'story'. Hence, one might better say 'According to a certain familiar mathematical fiction, $2 + 3 = 5$'.

Of course, a fictionalist then owes us two things. The first is an account of the operator 'According to the (mathematical) fiction ...' – and one which does not invoke fictional objects – existent or non-existent.[92] The second is an account of the phenomenology of mathematics – which certainly seems to deliver a relation between a subject and objects. The claim that there is complete reference failure here makes this a very tricky subject.[93] However, this is not the place to go into these matters.

3 Applied Mathematics

3.1 Introduction

In the previous sections, the subject of applied mathematics has surfaced a number of times – necessarily so, since the application of mathematics is one of its most notable features. An unavoidable question for mathematical pluralism is, then, what to make of this phenomenon? How is pure mathematics applied, and what – if anything – does this tell us about the nature of pure mathematics? In this section, we will look at the matter.

The subject is a crucial one. For a start, any account of pure mathematics which implies that it is not applicable, or even which leaves its applicability as an inexplicable mystery, is ipso facto inadequate. Moreover, a misunderstanding of the application of mathematics is liable to deliver a misunderstanding of pure mathematics. Thus, if one takes the truth of familiar

---

[91] See Field (1989), p. 3.

[92] On the metaphysics of fictional entities, see Kroon and Voltolini (2023).

[93] On issues of intentionality, see Jacob (2023).

mathematical statements to be established by their application (as, for example, did Quine), one will have to hold that there is a notion of mathematical truth that is not secundum quid. As is clear by now, I hold this to be a misunderstanding. These matters form the topic of this section.

In the first part of the section I will explain (with the help of a couple of examples) what it is to apply a pure mathematical structure. I will then hammer home the point that applied mathematics – even arithmetic – is an a posteriori matter. We will end with a look at what some notable philosophers of mathematics have said about applied mathematics.

3.2 The Application of Mathematics

But let us start by getting a few facts about applied mathematics straight. Pure mathematics is an investigation of mathematical structures in and of themselves. Applied mathematics is the use of such structures in the investigation of other things, in physics, economics, linguistics, or whatever. Of course, there is a connection between the two activities. For a start, some parts of pure mathematics (such as the original infinitesimal calculus) were developed specifically with an eye on their applications. But in principle, and even mostly in practice now, the two sorts of investigations are quite distinct.

Given mathematical pluralism, all mathematical structures, whatever their internal logic are, qua pure mathematical structures, equally correct. Matters of equal correctness are entirely different when we turn to applied mathematics. In this, a branch of mathematics or a mathematical structure is chosen and applied in an analysis of some natural or social phenomenon. There is then a question of which one is right – or at least which ones are better than others. (What exactly this means, we will come to in due course.) At any rate, mathematical structures are *not* all equally correct in this regard.

Thus, geometry has what one might call a canonical application: charting the structure of space (or maybe nowadays, space/time). For most of the history of mathematics it was assumed that Euclidean geometry was the correct geometry for that application; Euclidean geometry was developed for just that purpose. Indeed, in the history of mathematics until the nineteenth century it is hard to disentangle this geometry from its application. But of course, Kant notwithstanding, we now know better. The spatial structure of the cosmos is not Euclidean; it is not even one of constant curvature. Euclidean geometry was not the right geometry for the purpose. Naturally, a geometry can have many applications, and this by no means implies that Euclidean geometry is not the right geometry for some other application. What can be right for one application can be wrong for another, and vice versa. Thus, in quantum mechanics there are two well known kinds of statistics, Bose–Einstein and Fermi–Dirac, each of which implements a different kind of probability distribution for the entities involved.[94] And it turns out that the different kinds of statistics are appropriate for different kinds of particles. Bose–Einstein statistics works for bosons; Fermi–Dirac statistics works for fermions.

Hence, given any potential application, there is the question of which mathematical structure of a certain kind is best for the job. And conversely, given different mathematical structures of the same kind, there is the question of which application or applications they are appropriate for.

Indeed, there is a question of whether they have any applications at all. Some do not. There is, for example, as far as I know, no known application of the theory of large cardinals. And some branches of pure mathematics were found to have an application only well after their development: for example, the theory of electricity for complex numbers, and Special Relativity for group theory.

3.3 Two Examples

Against this background, we can now turn to the central question. How, exactly, does one apply a pure mathematical structure? Let us start with a couple of simple examples.

The first uses Ohm's law to determine the current in a circuit. Suppose we have a simple electrical circuit with a battery and a resistor.

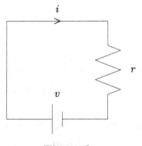

Figure 2

Suppose the voltage, v, produced by the battery is 6 volts, and the resistance, r, of the resistor is 2 ohms. What current, i (in amps), flows? Ohm's law, $v = ri$, tells us that it is 3. What is going on here?

---

[94] See, for example, French (2019).

First, we start with a state of affairs in the physical world. This will involve some wires and other bits of electrical paraphernalia. Understanding what is going on, and making predictions about it, will involve the following steps. (The sequence here is not a temporal one.) First, we need to invoke three (theoretical) physical quantities: the current flowing, I, the resistance, R, and the voltage in the circuit, V. Call the set of physical quantities, $\mathbb{P}$. Next, these have to be assigned some mathematical values. Hence, there are three functional expressions, μ_i, μ_r, μ_v, such that μ_i means 'the value in amps of', μ_r means 'the value in ohms of', and μ_v means 'the value in volts of'. (I will often omit the subscripts on 'μ' when they are clear from the context.) In our case, the mathematical values are real numbers, members of $\mathbb{R}$. So, the denotation of each μ is a map from $\mathbb{P}$ to $\mathbb{R}$. We can now enunciate Ohm's law:

- $\forall V, R, I(\mathcal{F}(V, R, I) \rightarrow \mu(V) = \mu(R) \times \mu(I))$

where $\mathcal{F}(V, R, I)$ states that V, R, and I are the quantities in an electrical circuit. Finally, we have to determine exactly how the mathematical entities and the operations on them work. In the case at hand, this is provided by the mathematical structure of the classical reals, $\mathfrak{R}$, $\langle \mathbb{R}, +, \times, 0, 1, < \rangle$.

Now, in our present example, we have three particular quantities, V_0, R_0, and I_0, such that $\mathcal{F}(V_0, R_0, I_0)$. Hence applying Ohm's law, we have $\mu(V_0) = \mu(R_0) \times \mu(I_0)$. We also have $\mu(V_0) = 6$ and $\mu(R_0) = 2$. If we now choose new terms, v, r, and i, for $\mu(V_0)$, $\mu(R_0)$, and $\mu(I_0)$, respectively, we have the equations:

- $v = r \times i$
- $v = 6$
- $r = 2$

Moving to the pure mathematical level, if these statements hold in $\mathfrak{R}$, then so does $i = 3$. So, moving back to the empirical level again, $\mu(I_0) = 3$. That is, the current in the circuit is 3 ohms.

Next, an example from economics.[95] According to standard microeconomics, other things being equal, in an equilibrium state, the price of a commodity is the point where supply and demand balance.

---

[95] There may well be, of course, important differences between the natural and the social sciences. As far as I can see, however, any such differences do not affect the points at issue here. Indeed, I choose an example from the social sciences precisely to show that the account of applied mathematics I am giving applies just as much to the social sciences as to the natural sciences.

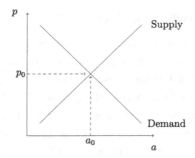

Figure 3

So, given some good, let p be the price per unit, and a be the amount produced. Suppose that for supply, $p = a$; and for demand, $p = 6 - a$. Then the equilibrium price per unit is given by the point $\langle p_0, a_0 \rangle$, where these lines cross; that is, p_0 is 3. What is going on here?

The situation we are dealing with concerns people who produce, and who buy and sell things. To understand the situation, we need to invoke two quantities, A, the amount produced, and P, the price. And $\mu(A) \in \mathbb{R}$ will be the amount of A in, say, kilograms; $\mu(P) \in \mathbb{R}$ will be the price in, say, dollars. But here we have two other things to consider, the causal relations of supply and demand between these quantities. Let these be S and D, respectively. Note that the appropriate mathematical structure is now the second-order reals, and $\mu(S)$ and $\mu(D)$ are relations between reals. That is, $\mu(S), \mu(D) \subseteq \mathbb{R}^2$. The law of supply and demand tells us that:

- $\forall A, P, S, D \, (\mathcal{F}(A, P, S, D) \rightarrow \forall x, y \, (\langle x, y \rangle \in \mu(S) \cap \mu(D) \rightarrow \mu(A) = x \wedge \mu(P) = y))$

where A and P are the equilibrium values, and $\mathcal{F}(A, P, S, D)$ states that the quantities concerned are in the appropriate relation (and we assume, for the sake of simplicity, that there is a unique point common to the two relations).

In the present situation, there are particular values, A_0, P_0, S_0, D_0, such that $\mathcal{F}(A_0, P_0, S_0, D_0)$. Hence, we know that $\forall x, y (\langle x, y \rangle \in \mu(S_0) \cap \mu(D_0) \rightarrow \mu(A_0) = x \wedge \mu(P_0) = y)$. We also know that $\mu(S_0) = \{\langle x, y \rangle : y = x\}$ and $\mu(D_0) = \{\langle y, x \rangle : y = 6 - x\}$. Let us now choose new terms a, p, s, d such that $s = \mu(S_0), d = \mu(D_0), a = \mu(A_0), p = \mu(P_0)$. Then we have the pure mathematical statement:

- $\forall x, y (\langle x, y \rangle \in \{\langle x, y \rangle : y = x\} \cap \{\langle y, x \rangle : y = 6 - x\} \rightarrow a = x \wedge p = y)$.

Ascending to this level, if this statement holds in $\mathfrak{R}$, then so does $p = 3$. That is, descending to the empirical level again, $\mu(P_0) = 3$. That is, the equilibrium price is 3 dollars per kilogram.

3.4 The General Picture and Its Ramifications

Bearing our examples in mind, I can now sketch the general situation involved in applying mathematics.[96] Let us call the topic to which we are applying mathematics, for want of a better phrase, the 'real world'. The real-world state of affairs will concern various real-world quantities. The situation describing these and the laws of nature can be expressed by a set of statements, D. If the descriptions involve numbers of various kinds, these descriptions will involve μ functional terms, but in applications of non-numerical mathematics, they will not. (I will give an example of this kind in the next section.) Pure mathematical statements, D', concerning some structure, $\mathfrak{A}$, are abstracted from these statements, ignoring the 'real world' interpretation of the mathematical quantities. Using what we know about $\mathfrak{A}$, we can infer some other statements, E', that hold in the structure. These can be 'de-abstracted', bringing the 'real world' interpretation back into the picture, to deliver some descriptions of the real-world situation, E. We may depict this as follows:

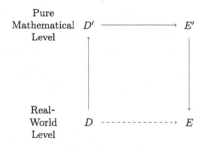

Figure 4

Hence it is that we can use the pure mathematical structure to infer facts about the 'real world'.

What takes us from D' to E' in this procedure is pure mathematics: proofs concerning $\mathfrak{A}$. The rest of the picture is a matter of empirical discovery. That this is so in the case of the scientific laws involved is, of course, clear. But the finding of an appropriate mathematical structure, $\mathfrak{A}$, is, in principle, equally an empirical discovery. This is exactly what the situation concerning the replacement of Euclidean geometry by Riemannian geometry showed us.

How does one determine the correct (or best) mathematical structure to be employed? First, statements at the real-world level are subject to direct empirical checks. Thus, if descriptions involve μ-sentences, they may be

---

[96] The basic idea of this is to be found in Priest (2005), 7.8.

subject to empirical testing by an appropriate measuring procedure.[97] For example, in the Ohm's law example, we can test the claim that $\mu(I_0) = 3$ by using an ammeter. So if the truth of this statement is already known, it may be explained. And if not, the procedure may be used to confirm or refute the application of machinery employed to get there.

Next, with regard to determining the correct mathematical structure to apply, note that a mathematical structure provides, in effect, a theory of how the real world things behave (as, for example, in the way that one may take the real numbers to give us a theory of the nature of spatio-temporal continua). A choice of mathematical structure is, then, a case of theory choice, to be determined by the usual criteria of such a choice. The first and most important criterion is adequacy to the data – which data are, as I have just explained, directly verifiable. However, generally speaking, this will not settle the issue, since other criteria – such as simplicity, unifying power, and so on – are also important. I will say more about these matters when I discuss the case of logical theory choice in the next section.

Of course, there is a question as to how such a theory is to be interpreted. One may be an instrumentalist and hold that we have but a calculating device for giving the right empirical results. However, if one is a realist about theoretical scientific entities – which I am inclined to be – there will be more to the story than this. The realist will hold that the mathematics gives the right empirical results because the mathematical structure tracks the physical structure in some appropriate sense.[98] That is, we can read off facts about the real world from the mathematics, since the two configurations have the same structure. That is, in our examples, 'μ' refers to a homomorphism. (It cannot be an isomorphism, since different physical quantities can have the same mathematical value.)[99]

Well, matters have to be a little more complicated than that. Often, the appropriate mathematical structure is much more than an instrumentalist black box, but the mathematical structure and the physical structure are not exactly the same. For example, the mathematics can be continuous while the physical system is discrete. Thus, in our example of supply and demand, the real numbers are continuous, but the quantities produced will normally be discrete. Or again: in the mathematics of fluid flow, continuous mathematics is used, but we know that the fluids are composed of molecules, and so are discrete.

---

[97] For a discussion of measurement in science, see Tal (2020).

[98] See, for example, Chakravartty (2017), 2.1.

[99] This is essentially the account defended by Pincock (2004), which he calls a *structuralist account*. His account, called by Bueno and Colyvan (2011) a *mapping account*, is subsumed by them in an account they call an *inferential account*. This has striking similarities to the account given here. (See esp. their diagram on p. 353.)

The mathematics may also ignore factors whose effect is below the level of empirical significance (such as, maybe, the gravitation effects of planets on the Sun).

In such cases, though the real-world and mathematical structures are not the same, the one approximates the other, at least to the order of magnitude with which we are concerned. How, exactly, to understand this matter is a somewhat tricky issue; but fortunately, one that we do not need to go into here.[100] Note, however, that we do not have to give a mathematical proof that the approximation is a good one. The fact that the application gives the right results to an appropriate level of accuracy provides an a posteriori demonstration that it does so.

Whatever one makes of all these matters is not relevant to the main point here, though, which is simply that one chooses the pure mathematical structure to apply which gives the best empirical results – however one theorises that matter.[101]

3.5 A Posteriori Mathematics

The example of geometry has already taught us that the pure mathematical structure to be employed in the step from D' to E' may not be the one we would have expected, might have to be revised in favour of something unexpected, and that what this is is an a posteriori matter. In this section, I want to dwell on the point further.

In the two examples of Section 3.3, the mathematical structure deployed was that of the standard reals. However, there is no a priori reason why this has to be the case. We might discover (or have discovered) that better predictions for electrical quantities are made using operations on the real numbers where multiplication is non-commutative. (Non-commutative operators, after all, play a significant role in the mathematics of quantum mechanics.) For example, this could be a structure $\mathfrak{R}' = \langle \mathbb{R}, +, \times', 0, 1, < \rangle$, $\times'$ being defined as follows:

- if $x > y$ then $x \times' y$ is $x \times y$
- if $y \geq x$ then $x \times' y$ is $x \times y - \frac{y-x}{r}$

where r is a large real number, representing, perhaps, some physical constant.

---

[100] For Pincock's discussion of the matter, see Pincock (2014).

[101] To this extent, matters are similar to a conventionalism of the kind advocated by Carnap's (1950) 'Empiricism, Semantics, and Ontology'. For him, too, there is a plurality of equally legitimate frameworks. Any choice between them is to be made on pragmatic grounds – such as which framework gives the right empirical predications.

Nor does the underlying logic of a structure applied have to be classical logic. There is no a priori reason why using the intuitionist reals might not give better predictions than using the classical reals. Let me make the point about using a mathematical structure with a non-classical logic with a more detailed, entirely hypothetical, example. This concerns (natural number) arithmetic[102] – which is, I think, the hardest kind of pure mathematical structure for which to envisage a structure different from the usual being applied.[103]

There are arithmetics (even axiomatic ones) which contain all the truths in the (classical) standard model of arithmetic, and then more. These are inconsistent, of course, but non-trivial. Their structure is now relatively well understood.[104] Take a simple one of these. In this, there is a tail, $\{0, 1, \dots n-1\}$, for some $n > 0$. The numbers in this behave consistently. Then, for $i \geq n$, the numbers cycle, so that for some period, $p > 0$, $i+p = i$ – and of course, $i+p \neq i$ too. We might depict the structure thus (where $\rightarrow$ is the successor function):

$$
\begin{array}{ccccccccc}
0 & \rightarrow & 1 & \rightarrow & \dots & \rightarrow & n & \rightarrow & n+1 \\
& & & & & & \uparrow & & \downarrow \\
& & & & & & n+p-1 & \leftarrow & \dots
\end{array}
$$

How might such an arithmetic come to be applied? Let us suppose that we predict a collision between a star and a huge planet. Using a standard technique, we compute their masses as x_1 and y_1. Since masses of this kind are, to within experimental error, the sum of the masses of the baryons (protons and neutrons) in them, it will be convenient to take a unit of measurement according to which a baryon has mass 1. In effect, therefore, these figures measure the numbers of baryons in the masses. After the collision, we measure the mass of the resulting (fused) body, and obtain the figure z, where z is much less than $x_1 + y_1$. Naturally, our results are subject to experimental error. But the difference is so large that it cannot possibly be explained by this. We check our instruments, suspecting a fault, but cannot find one; we check our computations for an error, but cannot find one.

Some days later, we have the chance to record another collision. We record the masses before the collision. This time they are x_2 and y_2. Again, after the

---

[102] I take this from Priest (2003).

[103] One might wonder how applying an arithmetical structure fits in to the schema I outlined earlier. Suppose, for example, that we have two bunches of objects, X and Y, we count each one, and then want to know how many things we have altogether. The 'laws of counting' tell us that $\mu(Z) = \mu(X) + \mu(Y)$, where $Z = X \cup Y$ and μ means 'the number of objects in'. Suppose that we have established that $\mu(X) = 3$ and $\mu(Y) = 12$. Then abstracting, we have: $z = x + y = 3 + 12$. Working in the pure mathematical abstract structure, we infer that $z = 15$. De-abstracting, we get $\mu(Z) = 15$, providing the answer.

[104] See, for example, Priest (1997b) and (2000).

collision, the mass appears to be z (the same as before), less than $x_2 + y_2$. The first result was no aberration.

We investigate various ways of solving the anomaly. We might revise the theories on which our measuring devices depend, but there may be no obvious way of doing this. We could say that some baryons disappeared in the collision; alternatively, we could suppose that under certain conditions the mass of a baryon decreases. But either of these options amounts to a rejection of the law of conservation of mass(-energy), which would seem to be a rather unattractive course of action.

Then we realise that the results can be accommodated by supposing that when we count baryons we may use a non-classical arithmetic. (As noted, we already know that different sorts of fundamental particles obey different statistics. Baryons are certain kinds of fermions.) The empirical results can be accommodated by using an inconsistent arithmetic of the kind just described, where z is the least inconsistent number, n, and $p = 1$.[105] For in such an arithmetic $x_1 + y_1 = x_2 + y_2 = z$, and our observations are explained without having to assume that the mass of baryons has changed, or that any are lost in the collisions.

The thought experiment can be continued in ways which make the application of an inconsistent arithmetic even more apt – indeed, even accommodating the fact that if $z' > z$, then $z' = z$ – but we do not need to go into the details here.[106] Of course, these facts can be accommodated in a consistent – though still highly non-standard – arithmetic. What you cannot have in such an arithmetic is the rest of standard arithmetic; or even the fragment axiomatised in Peano Arithmetic. And this rest may well be important in applying the arithmetic structure in further computations. At any rate, the point is made. There is nothing in principle against applying such a paraconsistent arithmetic.

Before I move on to comment on three philosophers whose writings deal with applied mathematics, let me summarise the picture of applied mathematics that has emerged in the preceding discussion. In applying mathematics, one uses a pure mathematical structure as depicted in the diagram of Subsection 3.4. The structure to be used is the one which gives the right empirical results (whatever that means). Sometimes, the pertinent pure mathematical structure will have arisen out of some kind of real-world practice,

---

[105] So the structure now looks like this:

$$0 \;\to\; 1 \;\to\; \ldots \;\to\; \overset{\curvearrowright}{n}$$

[106] They can be found in Priest (2003), §7.

making the distinction between the pure structure and a certain application almost invisible. (Euclidean geometry and natural-number arithmetic are cases in point.) That, however, provides no guarantee that a different structure will not do that job better. (Geometry again illustrates.) Sometimes, a certain sort of application will occasion the development of a whole new kind of pure mathematical structure which seems to be right for doing the job in question. (The infinitesimal calculus illustrates.) Many pure mathematical structures were, however, produced and investigated with no thought of application in mind. (The investigation of higher infinitudes is a case in point.) Though sometimes it will turn out, later, that such pure structures are just what seem to be required for a certain application. (Group theory and the Special Theory of Relativity provide a case in point.) Historically, then, the connection between pure and applied mathematics can be a somewhat tangled one. All the more reason to keep the fundamentals of the relation between them straight.

3.6 Comments on Three Philosophers

In the light of this discussion, let me comment on three notable philosophers of mathematics, pointing out where, in the light of the preceding account, they are right, and where they are wrong.

3.6.1 Quine

The first is Quine. Famously, according to Quine,[107] claims of pure mathematics are verified (established as true) holistically, together with our empirical scientific claims. And since they are true, and quantify over abstract mathematical objects, these exist.[108] The ontological claim, depending as it does on the view that anything quantified over in a true statement exists – at least if the language is an appropriately regimented one – is highly debatable.[109] But set that matter aside here and concentrate on just the epistemic claim.

It has many problems. The people who are best qualified to judge whether a claim of pure mathematics is true are pure mathematicians; and they care not at all about applications. What is important to them is proof. Next,

---

[107] Perhaps most notably in Quine (1951). See Colyvan (2001), esp. 2.5. For more on Quine's philosophy of mathematics see Hylton and Kemp (2019) and Priest (2010).

[108] This is sometimes known as 'Quine's indispensability argument': abstract entities exist because they are indispensable for science. See, for example, Colyvan (2001; 2019). Note that the plausibility of the ontological conclusion goes via the thought that we are justified in taking the statements to be true (simpliciter). The existence of a God is indispensable for Christian theology; but this provides no argument for the existence of God if the theological statements are not true.

[109] See Priest (2005).

as noted, there are important parts of pure mathematics that have (as yet) no empirical applications, such as the theory of large transfinite numbers, infinitary combinatorics, and the theory of surreal numbers.[110] Next, some theories can be applied in different areas. In some they are verified; in some, they would not be. Thus, the pure mathematical theory of the Lambek Calculus is verified when applied to grammatical parsing, but not when applied to simplifying Boolean electrical circuits. Does this mean that the pure mathematical statements are both true and false? Presumably not. As far as truth goes, one application would have to be privileged. But any such privileging is arbitrary.

But what underlies all these issues, as we may now see, is that the account simply has the wrong take on applied mathematics. What gets confirmed or otherwise by an application are the statements which describe the real world – the likes of our D and E in the diagram of Subsection 3.4. Application has no relevance to pure mathematical statements, like D' and E'. All that is confirmed or not in their application is whether they are the right bits of mathematics for the job at hand. The criterion of truth for statements like D' and E' is proof. And indeed, assuming the correctness of mathematical pluralism, this is truth *secundum quid*, truth-in-a-structure.[111]

3.6.2 Field

Let us now turn to Field. His *Science without Numbers*[112] is an essay on applied mathematics. The major explicit driver of Field's project is what he calls nominalism – perhaps better, anti-platonism: the view that no abstract entities, notably mathematical entities, exist. Field shows how an important example, Newtonian gravitational theory, may be formulated quantifying over only physical entities. In scientific practice, pure mathematics, which quantifies over abstract entities can be (and is) used, but this is a conservative extension of the physical machinery, and so is not involved essentially.[113] We are free, then, to adopt a fictionalist understanding of the pure mathematics. The pure mathematical statements are not really true. They are just 'true in the mathematical fiction' which is, say, $\Re$. (See Subsection 2.10.)

Field's view has some notable similarities to and notable differences with the view described earlier. To start with, I agree with Field's anti-platonism.

---

[110] On the last of these, see Knuth (1974).

[111] Hence the Quine indispensability argument also falters at the step that requires simple truth.

[112] Field (1980).

[113] In the way that non-finitary statements are used, according to Hilbert, in arithmetic. See Zach (2023).

However, as I have noted (2.10), I prefer a noneist approach to the matter. By all means, quantify over abstract entities. These are just non-existent objects.

Next, according to the two accounts of applied mathematics, the world (or an aspect of it) is described in empirical terms. We then interpret some of what is going on in pure mathematical terms and use the results of this to infer an empirical situation. There are three important differences between our approaches.

First, in my case, though not in Field's, the empirical statements refer to mathematical objects, such as numbers. However, I stress, and as I have already noted, these statements may be empirically verifiable by means of familiar measuring devices. (Nor do I regard the truth of such statements as committing to the existence of abstract entities, for reasons I have already noted.[114])

Secondly, as the introduction to the second edition of Field's book makes clear (see esp. p. P-4 ff.), there is another thought which drives his approach. Descriptions at the empirical level should make use of only intrinsic notions. How exactly to understand the notion of intrinsicality here is not a straightforward matter. But certainly the use of measuring scales and coordinate systems are not intrinsic. As is clear, my empirical level may make use of such notions. Now, I can understand the pull of intrinsicality from a certain theoretical perspective; but I think it fair to say that it is of virtually no importance for practicing (applied) mathematicians. If, in the end, science makes essential use of things such as measuring scales,[115] and this introduces an ineliminable conventionality into actual science, so be it.[116]

Third, it is important for Field that the application of the pure mathematics is conservative over the empirical level.[117] Conservativity plays no role in my account. Indeed, it is important that the result is not conservative. It is precisely this fact which allows for novel empirical predications, which can be used to test the machinery deployed. However, as just observed, Field and I understand different things by the empirical level.

Of course, making novel predications does play an important role in science, and Field is well aware of this. He is happy with the fact that in practice mathematical machinery is used to make novel predications. In principle, however, these could be obtained simply from the empirical base, from

---

[114] In the examples of Subsection 3.3, the empirical languages contained terms that refer to mathematical objects, though not quantification over them, for example, with things such as $\exists r\, r = \mu(I)$. The procedure I sketched carries over straightforwardly to such a syntax. The quantifiers are simply preserved in the abstracted pure mathematical statements (and back).

[115] So that they cannot be 'factored out' with invariance under the appropriate transformations.

[116] See the discussion of conventionalism in Tal (2020).

[117] One has to be a bit careful as to how to spell this out, though. See the discussion of conservativity in §0.4 of the second edition of the book.

which the appropriate mathematics may be thought of as abstracted via the appropriate representation theorem. His approach is therefore a sort of 'rational reconstruction', which mine is not.

3.6.3 Wigner

Finally, let us turn to Wigner's essay 'The Unreasonable Effectiveness of Mathematics in the Natural Sciences'.[118] As the title suggests, in this paper Wigner avers that we have no right to expect that mathematics can be effective in our engagement with the world. In a sense he's right; in a sense, he's wrong.

First, there is absolutely no a priori reason why the world should be ordered or have structure. It is entirely logically possible that the world should be as random as can be. And if it were, no mathematics would help to explain or predict events.

But of course, the world is not like this. We know that it has order – at least, pockets of it – because we are part of it, and we are ordered beings, as is our immediate environment. There is, then, at least in some sense, structure in the world. Mathematics is a science of structure (or structures); hence we can expect mathematics to get some grip on at least some aspects of the world.

Of course, there is no a priori reason why any particular mathematical structure should get a grip on it. But it is hardly surprising that some of the mathematics we have does so, since it evolved out of relevant practices, or was developed specifically for that purpose. That it does so is, then, no more surprising than that a telescope allows us to see at a distance, or that the flu vaccine protects against flu.

Naturally, it may turn out that the mathematics we have developed is the wrong mathematics for the project. As we know, it has been so sometimes in the past; and maybe it will be so again in the future. But if that turns out the be the case, people (or maybe, now, computers!) will at least attempt to design mathematics that works better.

Such development is certainly not the point of pure mathematics, which is to investigate interesting abstract structures in their own right. But designing pure mathematical structures for intended applications is obviously a legitimate project as well.

3.7 Conclusion

In this section, we have looked at the application of mathematics, and we have seen what goes on when a piece of pure mathematics is applied. Mathematical

---

[118] Wigner (1960).

pluralism delivers a natural picture of this, at odds with the way that the application of mathematics has frequently been thought of. In particular, only a notion of truth which is *secundum quid* is required by and/or justified by an application.

And with this, my discussion here of mathematical pluralism, as such, is completed. But it is clear that the view has connections with and implications for other areas of philosophy: metaphysics, epistemology, and, of course, logic. It is impossible to explore all these connections in an Element of this length – or even any one book. However, the connections with logic are particularly salient. In the next (and final) section of the Element I will explore some of these.

4 Matters of Logic

4.1 Introduction

This Element is about mathematics, not logic; but as is clear, logic has been lurking beneath the surface of much of the discussion. This is not the place for a comprehensive discussion of the nature of logic and related matters, but in this section I will discuss briefly the bearing of mathematical pluralism on some issues here.

Three will concern us. The first is the relationship between logic and applied mathematics. The second is logical pluralism. The third is non-classical logic. I will take up the matters in that order.

4.2 Logic as Applied Mathematics

As hardly needs to be said, contemporary logic uses mathematical techniques. It is not normally thought of as a branch of applied mathematics. That is exactly what an important and central part of it is, however. Let us see how.[119]

4.2.1 Pure and Applied Logic

Just as there is a distinction between pure and applied mathematics, there is a distinction between pure and applied logic. There is a multitude of pure logics (classical, intuitionist, paraconsistent, etc.) Each logic, $\mathfrak{L}$, will comprise a formal language, $\mathcal{L}$, a consequence relation, $\vdash$, defined on sentences of $\mathcal{L}$, and possibly other machinery. In general $\vdash \subseteq \wp(\mathcal{L}) \times \wp(\mathcal{L})$, but for our purposes we need be concerned only with consequence relations where the first component is a finite set, and the second is a singleton. A logic $\mathfrak{L}$ may be specified proof theoretically, model theoretically, algebraically, or in some other way.

---

[119] For further discussion, see Priest (202+b).

The pure mathematical structure may be used to establish the equivalence between different characterisations, and other important properties of ⊢, such as decidability or compactness.

A pure logic can have many applications. It may be applied to simplify electrical circuits (as with Boolean logic), or to parse sentences (as with the Lambek Calculus). But just as with geometry, logic has always had what one might call a canonical application: the analysis of arguments. These are arguments expressed in a vernacular language. When people argue, be they lawyers, politicians, historians, scientists, or wot not, they do not do so in a formal language. And, note, this is just as true of mathematicians. If you open the pages of a mathematics journal or textbook, you will not find the argument presented in *Principia*-ese, or any other formal language. People argue in a natural language (though some of the vocabulary used may be of a technical nature). The canonical application of a pure logic is to evaluate such arguments. That is what the subject was originally invented for.

4.2.2 The Canonical Application of a Pure Logic

How is this done? It precisely fits into the general schema of application given in Subsection 3.4.

Suppose we have an argument phrased in a vernacular language, $\mathcal{L}_V$. Let this have premises $\mathcal{P}_1, ... \mathcal{P}_n$, and conclusion C. We form the sentence:

- $\mathcal{A}_V$: the inference from $\mathcal{P}_1, ... \mathcal{P}_n$ to C is valid.

The sentences of the language are transformed into sentences $\mu(\mathcal{P}_1), ..., \mu(\mathcal{P}_n)$, $\mu(C)$ of $\mathcal{L}$; and $\mathcal{A}_V$ is transformed into the sentence:

- $\mathcal{A}$: $\mu(\mathcal{P}_1), ..., \mu(\mathcal{P}_n) \vdash \mu(C)$

The translation of vernacular sentences into $\mathcal{L}$ is done by a process that is usually informal, but teachers of elementary logic courses will normally spend a considerable amount of time developing the required skills in their students. The appropriate translation on some occasions may, itself, be a matter of theoretical contention. Thus, for example, the standard translation of a definite description is as a term of $\mathcal{L}$; but according to Russell's theory of definite descriptions, the whole sentence in which it occurs is translated into a sentence which contains no corresponding noun-phrase.

However, once this translation is made, the mathematical machinery of $\mathfrak{L}$ is applied to determine whether $\mathcal{A}$ holds in the pure mathematical structure. The sentence is then 'de-abstracted' back to the real-world level, to tell us whether $\mathcal{A}_V$ holds.

Refer back to the diagram of Subsection 3.4. The real-world level comprises vernacular arguments. *D* is a statement of validity for such an argument. *D'* is a corresponding mathematical statement of $\mathfrak{L}$ to be proven or refuted, and *E'* is the result. *E* is then the verdict for the original argument.

4.2.3 Pure Logic as Theory

As I noted in Subsection 3.4, when one applies a piece of pure mathematics to some real-world phenomenon, what one obtains is, in effect, a theory of how the things in that domain behave (though the theory may be subject to various possible interpretations, as I also discussed in Subsection 3.4). Thus, when a pure logic, $\mathfrak{L}$, is given its canonical application, it constitutes a theory of the validity or otherwise of inferences in the vernacular language (or the relevant fragment thereof).

Many such theories of (deductive) validity have been proposed, accepted, and/or rejected in the history of Western logic: Aristotelian syllogistic, medieval (and contemporary) connexive logic, medieval supposition theory, 'classical' logic, intuitionist logic, paraconsistent logics – to name but a few of the most obvious ones. And of course, different theories may give different verdicts on various inferences. Thus, if $\mathcal{A}_V$ concerns the inference:

- Donald Trump is corrupt and Donald Trump is not corrupt, so π is irrational

and $\mathfrak{L}$ is classical logic, then it will return the verdict *valid*. But if $\mathfrak{L}$ is a paraconsistent logic, it will return the verdict *invalid*.

Given a collection of different theories, the question – one which has played a major role in contemporary philosophy of logic – then arises as to which of them is rationally preferable.[120] Primary amongst the considerations for determining the answer is one of adequacy to the data. In the case of empirical theories, the data is provided by empirical observation and experimentation. In the case of logic it is provided by judgments about the validity or otherwise of particular inferences.[121] Thus:

[1] Mary is wearing a red dress and red shoes; so Mary is wearing a red dress

strikes us as valid, but:

---

[120] For a more extended discussion of the following, see Priest (2014) and (2016).
[121] Not, nota bene, forms of inference. These are always some kind of low-level theoretical generalisations.

[2] Mary is wearing either a red dress or red shoes; so Mary is wearing a red dress

strikes us as invalid. Getting these data points right is a mark in favour of a theory; getting them wrong is a mark against the theory.

Of course, as in the empirical sciences, data is not infallible. It can be wrong, and can be shown to be so by an otherwise good theory. Thus, an aberrant measurement in geometry may be taken to show that our measuring device, or our theory of how it works, is incorrect. Similarly, our naive judgments about the validity or otherwise of certain inferences may be wrong. 'Mary's dress is red, so Mary's dress is coloured' will strike most as valid. But standard logic says that it is not. What is valid is the inference with the extra premise 'Whatever is red is coloured'. Of course, simply writing off an aberrant data point is bad methodology. Some independent explanation needs to be found. In the case of the logic example, a natural such explanation is that we frequently do not mention obvious premises (such as that all red things are coloured) because they *are* obvious, and life is short.

In situations of any theoretical complexity, adequacy or otherwise to the data will not settle the matter. For a start, theories may be equally adequate or inadequate. In practice, other criteria are also important, such as simplicity, unifying power, non-reliance on ad hoc hypotheses, and so on. So it is in logic as well. Hence, the choice between different theories of this kind will bring into play, not only adequacy to the data, but other theoretical virtues.[122] How one aggregates all these factors will, then, be a crucial issue. However, we need not go into these matters further here. Suffice it to say that the theory it is most rational to accept is the one which performs best overall. What we have here is some kind of abductive inference.[123]

The important thing to observe at present is that rational choice of theory is a fallible and, in a certain sense, an a posteriori one. It is fallible because the data against which a theory is measured is itself fallible; and, moreover, new and better theories may appear at any time. It is a posteriori because its acceptability is to be judged in the light of data and methodological criteria, not given by certain and infallible rational intuition.

---

[122] In many cases, the mathematical structure, $\mathfrak{L}$, will contain machinery to be interpreted as truth, meaning, necessity, or some other vexed philosophical notion, when the structure receives its canonical interpretation. The theory of validity will then be embedded in a broader theory concerning, also, these notions. In this context, these other criteria will loom particularly large.

[123] See, further, Priest (2016; 2021a). This view is often now known as 'anti-exceptionalism'. I find this term both ugly and potentially misleading. I prefer 'abductivism'. For an application of this methodology in practice, see Berto et al. (2018).

This does not mean that one has to use sensory information. One can, of course, sometimes use such information to establish that an inference is invalid. For some inferences we may be able to see (literally) that the inference is invalid. For example, consider the inference:

- There are at least two people in the room; so there are a million people in the room.

where the inference concerns a certain room at a certain time. We may be able to see that the premise is true and the conclusion is not. But most cases will not be like this. One may judge that the inference is valid or invalid, merely by reflecting on it. In a similar way – though the analogy is not to be pushed too far – a native English speaker can simply reflect on the string of words 'The 45th President of the USA was corrupt', to see that it is grammatical, though that this is so is, of course, an a posteriori fact about English.

As with the application of a pure mathematical structure in any other area, then, finding the right pure logic for the canonical application is, as I argued in Subsections 3.4 and 3.5, an a posteriori matter, in the sense explained.

4.3 Logical Pluralism and Mathematical Pluralism

Let us turn to our second topic, namely logical pluralism.[124]

4.3.1 Logical Pluralism

Mathematical pluralism is the view that there are different pure mathematical structures – notably those based on different logics – which are, in an appropriate sense, equally legitimate. Correspondingly, logical pluralism is the view that there are different logics (consequence relations), which are, in an appropriate sense, equally legitimate. That claim can be understood in many ways, however; some of them quite innocuous; some of them highly contentious.[125] But, one might hold that mathematical pluralism entails logical pluralism in the following sense: there is no uniquely correct notion of validity to be used for the canonical application of logic. I do not think this follows, however, as I will now explain.[126] Whether the view is actually true is, of course, a different matter.

---

[124] This section reprises a theme developed in Priest (2021b).

[125] For a general discussion of logical pluralism see Priest (2006b), ch. 12, Russell (2019), and Stei (2023). The term 'logic' is itself highly ambiguous. A discussion of the ambiguity of the term can be found in Priest (2014).

[126] Shapiro (2014) holds that it does. This, we both agree, is the main difference between his view concerning mathematical pluralism and mine.

4.3.2 Truth Simpliciter and Truth in a Structure

The inference from mathematical pluralism to logical pluralism in this sense is a very straightforward one. When we reason about *ZFC* sets, classical logic is the correct logic to apply; when we reason about smooth infinitesimals, intuitionistic logic is the correct logic to apply; when we reason about inconsistent topologies, paraconsistent logic is the correct logic to apply. So each logic can be the correct one, depending on the context.[127]

It must be agreed that there is something right about this view. If we are reasoning about *ZFC* sets, it is appropriate to use classical logic; for this structure is closed under classical consequence. If we reason about smooth infinitesimals, it is appropriate to use intuitionistic logic; for this structure is closed under intuitionistic consequence. If we reason about inconsistent topologies, it is appropriate to use paraconsistent logic; for these structures are closed under paraconsistent consequence. Each logic is the correct logic for preserving truth-in-the-structure. It is the internal logic of the structure.

But the canonical application of logic is not about truth-in-a-structure-preservation. It is about truth-preservation. When we reason, we are interested in whether, given that our premises are true [or assuming them to be true] our conclusion is [would be] so as well. That the canonical application of logic is about truth preservation is not a profound claim; in some sense, it is a simple truism. Of course, it is a contentious matter as to how to spell out exactly what it means. Nor is it even clear what machinery is best employed to articulate the thought: proof procedures, set-theoretic interpretations, modal notions, probability theory? These matters are not pertinent here, though. The point is the simple distinction between truth-preservation, however one understands this notion, and the preservation of truth-in-a-structure. And once this distinction is noted, it is clear that the fact that there are different ways to preserve truth in a structure, depending on the structure, does not imply that there are many ways to preserve truth, simpliciter.

One way to make the point is as follows. Mathematical theories are not exactly stories, but they are much closer than one might have thought. In particular, when we reason about what holds in a mathematical structure, $\mathfrak{A}$, we, in effect, prefix our statements with the operator 'In structure $\mathfrak{A}$...'. (Of course, traditionally, mathematicians did not think of their statements as having this prefix. But that this is so is what mathematical pluralism appears to have shown us.) When we reason about what holds in a work of fiction, we, in effect, prefix our reasoning with the operator 'In fiction *F*...'. And in both cases, our

---

[127] The argument is run by Shapiro (2014)).

reasoning respects the internal logic of the structure/fiction – which does not have to be classical logic.[128] And truth-in-a-structure is not a species of truth simpliciter – any more than truth in a fiction is.

Another way of making the point is that any graspable and performable set of rules can be followed by an agent – rules of inference of some logical theory included. This obviously does not validate logical pluralism in the required sense. For logic, following the rules must have a certain point – truth-preservation is the traditional and correct candidate.

4.3.3 Objections

The preceding argument deploys the distinction between truth and truth-in-a-structure. How might one challenge this?

One way is as follows. Truth preservation simpliciter is validity. Validity is truth preservation in all interpretations. Interpretations are the same thing as structures. So preservation of truth is the same thing as preservation of truth-in-a-structure.

Several issues would have to be addressed to make this argument cogent. One would need to defend a model-theoretic account of validity. One would have to face the fact that in many pure logics validity is not defined in terms of truth preservation, but in some other terms. (For example, in many-valued logics it is defined in terms of the preservation of designated values.) And one would have to defend the anything but obvious claim that structures and interpretations are the same thing. (See Subsection 2.5.)

But even assuming that these points can be adequately addressed, there is a simple and obvious problem with the objection. Model-theoretic validity is not truth-preservation in all interpretations. Different logics (intuitionist, classical, paraconsistent, etc.) have different *kinds* of interpretations. Their model theories therefore provide an understanding of truth preservation in the appropriate kind of structure – the internal logic of the structure – not validity simpliciter. And if one really defines validity as truth-preservation in *all* interpretations, then, given the plurality of formal logics on which mathematical structures may be based, the logic will amount, as near as makes no difference, to the null logic: no inference is valid. Such would clearly make validity useless for evaluating the validity of ordinary arguments, and so cannot be right.

A second way to challenge the distinction between truth and truth-in-a-structure might be as follows. That validity is about truth preservation is, in

---

[128] For a fiction in which the internal logic is a paraconsistent logic, see the short story 'Sylvan's Box', Priest (1997a).

the sense we have been dealing with, a banal claim. It is an equally banal claim that truth, whatever it is, is determined by reality. And isn't reality just another structure? So reasoning about truth is simply a variety of reasoning about truth-in-a-structure. In some sense, I suppose, reality is a structure, or at least, has a structure. But it's not just any old structure. It is highly privileged. I ask you whether it is true that there were more people at Trump's presidential inauguration than at Obama's. I don't need to tell you that I want an answer that corresponds to reality.

One way to see the point is this. We have both been reading Conan Doyle's *The Hound of the Baskervilles*. We argue about whether Holmes used a Colt revolver. I say he did. You say he used a Smith and Wesson. Of course, neither of us thinks that our claims are literally true: Doyle's text is just a fiction. We are both tacitly prefixing our claims with 'In *The Hound of the Baskervilles*...'. We just omit this because, given the mutually understood context, it is unnecessary.

Now, by contrast, if I ask you whether Trump's crowd was bigger than Obama's, and you say, 'No, the crowd was much smaller', I don't have to understand you as saying '*In reality*, the crowd was much smaller'; and if you did, the prefix would be entirely otiose. Reality, then, is not simply a structure, on a par with other structures.

The distinction between truth-in-a-structure and truth simpliciter, then, stands; and this distinction bars the way from mathematical pluralism to the logical pluralism in question.

4.4 Non-Classical Logic

Let us turn to our third topic. The distinction between the preservation of truth in a structure and validity is relevant to another claim that has recently been made. Williamson (2018) has argued that the application of mathematics in science provides a strong argument for the correctness of classical logic. The argument is essentially as follows.

Pure mathematics is based on classical logic, and therefore deploys the classical notion of validity, including essentially inferential moves that fail in a sub-classical logic. The fact that mathematics has been so successfully applied in science therefore speaks strongly in favour of the classical notion of validity, and against a non-classical notion – or at the very least, an advocate of a non-classical notion of validity owes us an account of this successful application. He puts the point as follows:[129]

---

[129] Williamson (2018), p. 399. His italics.

> The hardest test of logic is mathematics, which constitutes by far the most sustained and successful deductive enterprise in human history. With only minor exceptions, mathematicians have freely relied on *classical logic*, including principles such as the law of excluded middle, $A \lor \neg A$. They unquestioningly accept classical reasoning in proofs. When deviant logicians reject a classical principle, they face an obvious challenge: what does this mean for mathematics? Where does this leave theorems whose proofs rely solely on the principle?

The claim that pure mathematics is based on classical logic is not, of course, one that a mathematical pluralist will grant; as we have seen, there is perfectly good pure mathematics that uses a non-classical logic. But Williamson clearly has applied mathematics in his sights. However, as the account of the application of mathematics of the last section shows, this does little to help his case. Williamson is assuming that one must take the inferences involved in applying mathematics to be valid. That is, they preserve truth simpliciter. But they do not: they involve the preservation of truth-in-a-structure, for the structures in question. In itself, this shows nothing about validity. As we have seen, that is a different matter. If, when we reason about what holds in the structure $\mathfrak{A}$, we use the inference $A \vdash B$, we endorse the claim that 'In $\mathfrak{A}$, A' entails 'In $\mathfrak{A}$, B'. This does not imply that A entails B. 'In $\mathfrak{A}$, C' is neither necessary nor sufficient for C. (If, as I shall note in a moment, for two hundred years, physics, in the form of the infinitesimal calculus, used a paraconsistent inference procedure because of the use of infinitesimals, Williamson would not, I am sure, infer that paraconsistent logic was correct. He would, I presume, take an infinitesimal to be some kind of felicitous computational, ideal, or approximating object.)

Even more to the point, the premise of Williamson's argument, that the mathematics that has been applied 'has relied on' classical logic, is untenable. For a start, it is anachronistic. Mathematics has been applied for millennia, and classical (aka Frege/Russell) logic was invented only just over 100 years ago. Of course, mathematicians reasoned before that; but the reasoning was informal and did not answer to any formal logic.

What's more, at times, applied mathematicians clearly flouted the principles of classical logic. For example, the reasoning that was applied in the infinitesimal calculus from its discovery/invention till the nineteenth century could not have endorsed Explosion, since it assumed that infinitesimals behaved in a contradictory fashion.[130] Of course, we now know how to formalise this bit of mathematics using classical logic. Maybe it is even true

---

[130] See Brown and Priest (2004) and Sweeney (2014).

that all the mathematics that has been applied can be formalised using classical logic, but that tells us little. It can be formalised in other ways too. For example, the whole of Zermelo–Fraenkel set theory can be understood using the paraconsistent logic *LP*.[131] Moreover, once one leaves the domain of the natural sciences, it is now common for non-classical logics to be deployed. Linguists frequently appeal to logics with truth value gaps to analyse presupposition, and to fuzzy logics to analyse things like gradable adjectives.[132] Moreover, this says nothing of the use by logicians and linguists of non-classical logics to analyse self-reference.

Finally, even if it *were* the case that, historically, only mathematics based on classical logic had ever been applied, it might fairly be claimed that this is entirely accidental and due to the fact that the varieties of non-classical mathematics had not yet been developed. As the example of linguistics shows, non-classical logic *is* now being applied. Even if one were to concede that mathematics based on non-classical logic has not thus far been deployed in the natural sciences, it is quite within the bounds of possibility that it will be. If it is found to give the right results, it will be. The application of mathematics and its history is therefore of little help to the defender of 'classical' logic.

4.5 Conclusion

So much for a somewhat whistle-stop tour of some logical issues. This brings the Element's discussions to a closure. Of necessity (given the word limit on Elements in this series), it has been relatively swift. There is much more to be said about the issues traversed; and I have no doubt that much more will be said by logicians and philosophers of mathematics. But I hope that the Element has at least laid out clearly the basics of mathematical pluralism and thus laid the ground for future discussions. All that remains is to say a few concluding words.

---

[131] See, for example, Priest (2006a), 18.4, and Priest (2017), sect. 11.

[132] See, for example, Gregory (2015). As the book's blurb says: 'This book will take linguistics students beyond the classical logic used in introductory courses into the variety of non-standard logics that are commonly used in research'.

Postface

Like it or not, the plurality of mathematics seems to be a fact of contemporary mathematical life. Ours it is to make sense of this fact. One can, if one wishes, declare that there is one true mathematics (*ZFC?*) and that the rest is all mistaken. Such would seem to be a procrustean position of desperate proportions. Mathematical pluralism, as I have sketched it, is, I hope, a much more plausible view than this. There is a genuine plurality of pure mathematical practices, each with its own set of rules. As Wittgenstein says:[133]

> I should like to say: mathematics is a MOTLEY of techniques of proof.—
> And upon this is based its manifold applicability and its importance.

Moreover, we may legitimately pursue any of the practices. All pure mathematical animals are equal. Though, of course, in terms of intrinsic interest, richness, beauty, application, and so on, there will be significant differences. Some of these animals will always be more equal than others.

---

[133] Wittgenstein (1967), p. 84e. His capitals.

References

Avron, A. (2010), 'A New Approach to Predicative Set Theory', pp. 31–64 of R. Schindler (ed.), *Ways of Proof Theory*, Heisenstamm: Ontos Verlag.

Balaguer, M. (1995), 'A Platonist Epistemology', *Synthese* 103: 303–25.

Balaguer, M. (2018), 'Fictionalism in the Philosophy of Mathematics', in E. Zalta (ed.), *Stanford Encyclopedia of Philosophy*, https://plato.stanford.edu/entries/fictionalism-mathematics/.

Beall, J. (1999), 'From Full Blooded Platonism to Really Full Blooded Platonism', *Philosophia Mathematica* 7: 322–5.

Bell, J. (2008), *A Primer of Infinitesimal Analysis*, 2nd ed., Cambridge: Cambridge University Press.

Bell, J. (2022), 'Continuity and Infinitesimals', in E. Zalta (ed.), *Stanford Encyclopedia of Philosophy*, https://plato.stanford.edu/entries/continuity/.

Benacerraf, P. (1965), 'What Numbers Could not Be', *Philosophical Review* 74: 47–73.

Berto, F., French, R., Priest, G., and Ripley, D. (2018), 'Williamson on Counterpossibles', *Journal of Philosophical Logic* 47: 693–713.

Brady, R. (1989), 'The Non-Triviality of Dialectical Set Theory', pp. 437–71 of G. Priest, R. Routley, and J. Norman (eds.), *Paraconsistent Logic: Essays on the Inconsistent*, Munich: Philosophia Verlag.

Bridges, D. (2013), 'Constructive Mathematics', in E. Zalta (ed.), *Stanford Encyclopedia of Philosophy*, https://plato.stanford.edu/entries/mathematics-constructive/.

Bridges, D., and Richman, F. (1987), *Varieties of Constructive Mathematics*, Cambridge: Cambridge University Press.

Brown, B., and Priest, G. (2004), 'Chunk and Permeate, a Paraconsistent Inference Strategy; Part I, the Infinitesimal Calculus', *Journal of Philosophical Logic* 22: 379–88.

Bueno, O. (2011), 'Relativism in Set Theory and Mathematics', pp. 553–68 of S. Hales (ed.), *A Companion to Relativism*, Oxford: Wiley-Blackwell.

Bueno, O., and Colyvan, M. (2011), 'An Inferential Conception of the Application of Mathematics', *Noûs* 45: 345–74.

Carnap, R. (1950), 'Empiricism, Semantics and Ontology', *Revue Internationale de Philosophie* 4: 20–40; reprinted as pp. 205–21 of *Meaning and Necessity: a Study in Semantics and Modal Logic*, 2nd ed., Chicago: University of Chicago Press, 1956.

Chakravartty, A. (2017), 'Scientific Realism', in E. Zalta (ed.), *Stanford Encyclopedia of Philosophy*, https://plato.stanford.edu/entries/scientific-realism/.

Clarke-Doane, J. (2022), *Mathematics and Metaphilosophy*, Cambridge: Cambridge University Press.

Colyvan, M. (2001), *The Indispensability of Mathematics*, New York: Oxford University Press.

Colyvan, M. (2019), 'Indispensability Arguments in the Philosophy of Mathematics', in E. Zalta (ed.), *Stanford Encyclopedia of Philosophy*, https://plato.stanford.edu/entries/mathphil-indis/.

Cotnoir, A., and Weber, Z. (2015), 'Inconsistent Boundaries', *Synthese* 192: 1267–94.

Crosilla, L. (2019), 'Set Theory: Constructive and Intuitionist *ZF*', in E. Zalta (ed.), *Stanford Encyclopedia of Philosophy*, https://plato.stanford.edu/entries/set-theory-constructive/.

Curry, H. (1951), *Outlines of a Formalist Philosophy of Mathematics*, Amsterdam: North-Holland.

Da Costa, N. (1974), 'On the Theory of Inconsistent Formal Systems', *Notre Dame Journal of Formal Logic* 15: 497–509.

Davies, E. B. (2005), 'A Defence of Mathematical Pluralism', *Philosophia Mathematica* 13: 252–76.

Doherty, F. (2017), 'Hilbert on Consistency as a Guide to Mathematical Reality', *Logique et Analyse* 237: 107–28.

Dummett, M. (2000), *Elements of Intuitionism*, 2nd ed., Oxford: Oxford University Press.

Eklund, M. (2019), 'Fictionalism', in E. Zalta (ed.), *Stanford Encyclopedia of Philosophy*, https://plato.stanford.edu/entries/fictionalism/.

Enderton, H. (1977), *Elements of Set Theory*, New York: Academic Press.

Engeler, E., and Röhrl, H. (1969), 'On the Problems of Foundations of Category Theory', *Dialectica* 23: 58–66.

Field, H. (1980), *Science without Numbers*, Oxford: Oxford University Press; 2nd ed., 2016.

Field, H. (1989), 'Introduction: Fictionalism, Epistemology, and Modality', ch. 1 of *Realism, Mathematics, and Modality*, Oxford: Basil Blackwell.

French, S. (2019), 'Identity and Individuality in Quantum Theory', in E. Zalta (ed.), *Stanford Encyclopedia of Philosophy*, https://plato.stanford.edu/entries/qt-idind/.

Friend, M. (2014), *Pluralism in Mathematics: A New Position in Philosophy of Mathematics*, Dordrecht: Springer.

Gregory, H. (2015), *Language and Logics: An Introduction to the Logical Foundations of Language*, Edinburgh: Edinburgh University Press.

Hájek, P., and Haniková, Z. (2003), 'A Development of Set Theory in Fuzzy Logic', pp. 273–85 of M. Fitting and E. Orłowska (eds.), *Beyond Two: Theory and Applications of Multiple-Valued Logic*, Heidelberg: Springer.

Hallett, M. (2013), 'Zermelo's Axiomatization of Set Theory', in E. Zalta (ed.), *Stanford Encyclopedia of Philosophy*, https://plato.stanford.edu/entries/zermelo-set-theory/.

Hamkins, J. (2012), 'The Set-Theoretic Multiverse', *Review of Symbolic Logic* 5: 416–49.

Hamkins, J. (2020), *Lectures on the Philosophy of Mathematics*, Cambridge, MA: Massachusetts Institute of Technology Press.

Hamkins. J. (2023), 'Skolem's Paradox', *Infinitely More*, https://www.infinitelymore.xyz/p/skolems-paradox.

Hamkins, J., and Yang, R. (2013), 'Satisfaction is Not Absolute', *arXiv*: 1312.0670, https://arxiv.org/abs/1312.0670.

Hatcher, W. (1982), *The Logical Foundations of Mathematics*, Oxford: Pergamon Press.

Hellman, G., and Bell, J. (2006), 'Pluralism and the Foundations of Mathematics', pp. 64–79 of C. Waters, H. Longino, and S. Kellert (eds.), *Scientific Pluralism*, Minneapolis: University of Minnesota Press.

Holmes, M. (2017), 'Alternative Axiomatic Set Theories', in E. Zalta (ed.), *Stanford Encyclopedia of Philosophy*, https://plato.stanford.edu/entries/settheory-alternative/#AckeSetTheo.

Horsten, L. (2017), 'Philosophy of Mathematics', *Stanford Encyclopedia of Philosophy*, http://plato.stanford.edu/entries/philosophy-mathematics.

Hylton, P., and Kemp, G. (2019), 'Willard Van Orman Quine', in E. Zalta (ed.), *Stanford Encyclopedia of Philosophy*, https://plato.stanford.edu/entries/quine/.

Iemhoff, R. (2013), 'Intuitionism in the Philosophy of Mathematics', in E. Zalta (ed.), *Stanford Encyclopedia of Philosophy*, https://plato.stanford.edu/entries/intuitionism/.

Irvine, A. (2015), '*Principia Mathematica*', in E. Zalta (ed.), *Stanford Encyclopedia of Philosophy*, https://plato.stanford.edu/entries/principia-mathematica/.

Jacob, P. (2023), 'Intentionality', in E. Zalta (ed.), *Stanford Encyclopedia of Philosophy*, https://plato.stanford.edu/entries/intentionality/.

Koellner P. (2009), 'Truth in Mathematics: The Question of Pluralism', pp. 80–116 of O. Bueno and Ø. Linnebo (eds.), *New Waves in Philosophy of Mathematics: New Waves in Philosophy*, London: Palgrave Macmillan.

Koellner, P. (2010), 'Independence and Large Cardinals', in E. Zalta (ed.), *Stanford Encyclopedia of Philosophy*, https://plato.stanford.edu/entries/independence-large-cardinals/.

Koellner, P. (2013), 'Large Cardinals and Determinacy', in E. Zalta (ed.), *Stanford Encyclopedia of Philosophy*, https://plato.stanford.edu/entries/large-cardinals-determinacy/.

Knuth, D. (1974), *Surreal Numbers*, Reading, MA: Addison-Wesley.

Kroon, F., and Voltolini, A. (2023), 'Fictional Entities', in E. Zalta (ed.), *Stanford Encyclopedia of Philosophy*, https://plato.stanford.edu/entries/fictional-entities/.

Kunen, K. (1980), *Set Theory: An Introduction to Independence Proofs*, Amsterdam: North Holland.

Levy, A. (1979), *Basic Set Theory*, Berlin: Springer.

Maddy, P. (1997), *Naturalism in Mathematics*, Oxford: Oxford University Press.

Maddy, P. (2007), *Second Philosophy: A Naturalistic Method*, Oxford: Oxford University Press.

Marquis, J.-P. (2014), 'Category Theory', in E. Zalta (ed.), *Stanford Encyclopedia of Philosophy*, https://plato.stanford.edu/entries/category-theory/.

McCarty, D. (1991), 'Incompleteness in Intuitionist Mathematics', *Notre Dame Journal of Formal Logic* 32: 323–58.

Miller, A., and Sultanescu, O. (2022), 'Rule Following and Intentionality', in E. Zalta (ed.), *Stanford Encyclopedia of Philosophy*, https://plato.stanford.edu/entries/rule-following/.

Mortensen, C. (1995), *Inconsistent Mathematics*, Dordrecht: Kluwer.

Mortensen, C. (2010), *Inconsistent Geometry*, London: College Publications.

Mortensen, C. (2017), 'Inconsistent Mathematics', in E. Zalta (ed.), *Stanford Encyclopedia of Philosophy*, https://plato.stanford.edu/entries/mathematics-inconsistent/.

Moss, L. (2018), 'Non-wellfounded Set Theory', in E. Zalta (ed.), *Stanford Encyclopedia of Philosophy*, https://plato.stanford.edu/entries/nonwellfounded-set-theory/.

Petersen, U. (2000), 'Logic without Contraction and Based on Unrestricted Abstraction', *Studia Logica* 64: 365–403.

Pincock, C. (2004), 'A New Perspective on the Problem of Applying Mathematics', *Philosophia Mathematica* 12: 135–61.

Pincock, C. (2014), 'How to Avoid Inconsistent Idealizations', *Synthese* 191: 2957–72.

Posy, C. (2020), *Mathematical Intuitionism*, Cambridge: Cambridge University Press.

Priest, G. (1973), 'A Bedside Reader's Guide to the Conventionalist Philosophy of Mathematics', pp. 115–32 of J. Bell, J. Cole, G. Priest, and A. Slomson (eds.), *Proceedings of the Bertrand Russell Memorial Logic Conference, Denmark 1971*, Leeds: University of Leeds.

Priest, G. (1997a), 'Sylvan's Box', *Notre Dame Journal of Formal Logic* 38: 573–82; reprinted as §6.6 of Priest (2005).

Priest, G. (1997b), 'Inconsistent Models of Arithmetic, I: Finite Models', *Journal of Philosophical Logic* 26: 1519–25.

Priest, G. (1998), 'Number', pp. 47–54, Vol. 7, of E. Craig (ed.), *Encyclopedia of Philosophy*, London: Routledge.

Priest, G. (2000), 'Inconsistent Models of Arithmetic, II: The General Case', *Journal of Symbolic Logic* 65: 223–35.

Priest, G. (2003), 'On Alternative Geometries, Arithmetics, and Logics: A Tribute to Łukasiewicz', *Studia Logica* 74: 441–68.

Priest, G. (2005), *Towards Non-Being*, Oxford: Oxford University Press; 2nd ed., 2016.

Priest, G. (2006a), *In Contradiction*, 2nd ed., Oxford: Oxford University Press.

Priest, G. (2006b), 'Logical Pluralism', ch. 12 of *Doubt Truth to be a Liar*, Oxford: Oxford University Press.

Priest, G. (2010), 'Quine: Naturalism Unravelled', pp. 19–30 of M. Dumitru and C. Stoenescu (eds.), *Cuvinte, Teorii si Lucruri: Quine in Perspectiva*, Bucharest: Editura Pelican.

Priest, G. (2013a), 'Mathematical Pluralism', *Logic Journal of IGPL* 21: 4–14.

Priest, G. (2013b), 'Indefinite Extensibility: Dialetheic Style', *Studia Logica* 101: 1263–75.

Priest, G. (2014), 'Revising Logic', ch. 12 of P. Rush (ed.), *The Metaphysics of Logic*, Cambridge: Cambridge University Press.

Priest, G. (2016), 'Logical Disputes and the *a Priori*', *Logique et Analyse* 236: 347–66.

Priest, G. (2017), 'What If? The Exploration of an Idea', *Australasian Journal of Logic* 14(1): Article 4, https://ojs.victoria.ac.nz/ajl/article/view/4028/3574.

Priest, G. (2019a), 'From the Foundations of Mathematics to Mathematical Pluralism', pp. 363–80 of S. Centrone, D. Kant, and D. Sarikaya (eds.), *Reflections on the Foundations of Mathematics: Univalent Foundations, Set Theory and General Thoughts*, New York: Springer.

Priest, G. (2019b), 'Gödel's Theorem and Paraconsistency', in E. Almeida, A. Costa-Leite, and R. Freire (eds.), *Lógica no Avião*, http://lna.unb.br/lna_n01_01_gpriest.pdf.

Priest, G. (2021a), 'Logical Abductivism and Non-Deductive Inference', *Synthese* 199: 3207–17.

Priest, G. (2021b), 'A Note on Mathematical Pluralism and Logical Pluralism', *Synthese* 198: 4937–46.

Priest, G. (202+a), 'How Do You Apply Mathematics?', *Axiomathes*, forthcoming.

Priest, G. (202+b), 'Logic as Applied Mathematics: With Application to the Notion of Logical Form', to appear.

Priest, G., Berto, F., and Weber, Z. (2022), 'Dialetheism', in E. Zalta (ed.), *Stanford Encyclopedia of Philosophy*, https://plato.stanford.edu/entries/dialetheism/.

Priest, G., Tanaka, K., and Weber, Z. (2022), 'Paraconsistent Logic', in E. Zalta (ed.), *Stanford Encyclopedia of Philosophy*, https://plato.stanford.edu/entries/logic-paraconsistent/.

Quine, W. (1951), 'Two Dogmas of Empiricism', *Philosophical Review* 60: 20–43; reprinted as ch. 2 of *From a Logical Point of View*, Cambridge, MA: Harvard University Press.

Reck, E., and Schiemer, G. (2019), 'Structuralism in the Philosophy of Mathematics', in E. Zalta (ed.), *Stanford Encyclopedia of Philosophy*, https://plato.stanford.edu/entries/structuralism-mathematics/.

Reicher, M. (2019a), 'Alexius Meinong', in E. Zalta (ed.), *Stanford Encyclopedia of Philosophy*, https://plato.stanford.edu/entries/meinong/.

Reicher, M. (2019b), 'Non-Existent Objects', in E. Zalta (ed.), *Stanford Encyclopedia of Philosophy*, https://plato.stanford.edu/entries/nonexistent-objects/.

Russell, G. (2019), 'Logical Pluralism', in E. Zalta (ed.), *Stanford Encyclopedia of Philosophy*, https://plato.stanford.edu/entries/logical-pluralism/.

Sambin, G. (2011), 'A Minimalist Foundation at Work', ch. 4 of D. DeVidi, M. Hallett, and P. Clarke (eds.), *Logic, Mathematics, Philosophy, Vintage Enthusiasms: Essays in Honour of John L. Bell*, Heidelberg: Springer.

Shapiro, S. (2004), 'Foundations of Mathematics: Ontology, Epistemology, Structure', *Philosophical Quarterly* 54: 16–37.

Shapiro, S. (2014), *Varieties of Logic*, Oxford: Oxford University Press.

Stei, E. (2023), *Logical Pluralism and Logical Consequence*, Cambridge: Cambridge University Press.

Sweeney, D. (2014), 'Chunk and Permeate: The Infinitesimals of Isaac Newton', *History and Philosophy of Logic* 35: 1–23.

Takeuti, G. (1981), 'Quantum Set Theory', pp. 303–22 of E. Beltrametti and B. van Fraassen (eds.), *Current Issues in Quantum Logic*, New York: Plenum.

Tal, E. (2020), 'Measurement in Science', in E. Zalta (ed.), *Stanford Encyclopedia of Philosophy*, https://plato.stanford.edu/entries/measurement-science/.

Tennant, N. (2017), 'Logicism and Neologicism', in E. Zalta (ed.), *Stanford Encyclopedia of Philosophy*, https://plato.stanford.edu/entries/logicism/.

Van Atten, M. (2017), 'The Development of Intuitionist Logic', in E. Zalta (ed.), *Stanford Encyclopedia of Philosophy*, https://plato.stanford.edu/entries/intuitionistic-logic-development/.

Warren, J. (2015), 'Conventionalism, Consistency, and Consistency Sentences', *Synthese* 192: 1351–71.

Weber, Z. (2010), 'Transfinite Numbers in Paraconsistent Set Theory', *Review of Symbolic Logic* 3: 71–92.

Weber, Z. (2012), 'Transfinite Cardinals in Paraconsistent Set Theory', *Review of Symbolic Logic* 5: 269–93.

Weber, Z. (2021), *Paradoxes and Inconsistent Mathematics*, Cambridge: Cambridge University Press.

Weber, Z. (2022), *Paraconsistency in Mathematics*, Cambridge: Cambridge University Press.

Weir, A. (2019), 'Formalism in the Philosophy of Mathematics', *Stanford Encyclopedia of Philosophy*, http://plato.stanford.edu/entries/formalism-mathematics/.

Wigner, E. (1960), 'The Unreasonable Effectiveness of Mathematics in the Natural Sciences', *Communications on Pure and Applied Mathematics* 13: 1–14.

Williamson, T. (2018), 'Alternative Logics and Applied Mathematics', *Philosophical Issues* 28: 399–424.

Wittgenstein, L. (1953), *Philosophical Investigations*, Oxford: Basil Blackwell.

Wittgenstein, L. (1964), *Philosophical Remarks*, Oxford: Basil Blackwell.

Wittgenstein, L. (1967), *Remarks on the Foundations of Mathematics*, Cambridge: Massachusetts Institute of Technology Press.

Zach, R. (2023), 'Hilbert's Program', in E. Zalta (ed.), *Stanford Encyclopedia of Philosophy*, https://plato.stanford.edu/entries/hilbert-program/.

Zalta, E. (2016), 'Frege', in E. Zalta (ed.), *Stanford Encyclopedia of Philosophy*, https://plato.stanford.edu/entries/frege/.

Zalta, E. (2023), 'Mathematical Pluralism', *Noûs*, https://onlinelibrary.wiley.com/doi/full/10.1111/nous.12451.

Acknowledgments

This Element is dedicated, with pleasure, to Hartry Field and Stewart Shapiro, two dear friends and fellow philosophers of mathematics, with much thanks for many happy years of agreement and disagreement.

Cambridge Elements ≡

The Philosophy of Mathematics

Penelope Rush
University of Tasmania

From the time Penny Rush completed her thesis in the philosophy of mathematics (2005), she has worked continuously on themes around the realism/anti-realism divide and the nature of mathematics. Her edited collection *The Metaphysics of Logic* (Cambridge University Press, 2014), and forthcoming essay 'Metaphysical Optimism' (*Philosophy Supplement*), highlight a particular interest in the idea of reality itself and curiosity and respect as important philosophical methodologies.

Stewart Shapiro
The Ohio State University

Stewart Shapiro is the O'Donnell Professor of Philosophy at The Ohio State University, a Distinguished Visiting Professor at the University of Connecticut, and a Professorial Fellow at the University of Oslo. His major works include *Foundations without Foundationalism* (1991), *Philosophy of Mathematics: Structure and Ontology* (1997), *Vagueness in Context* (2006), and *Varieties of Logic* (2014). He has taught courses in logic, philosophy of mathematics, metaphysics, epistemology, philosophy of religion, Jewish philosophy, social and political philosophy, and medical ethics.

About the Series

This Cambridge Elements series provides an extensive overview of the philosophy of mathematics in its many and varied forms. Distinguished authors will provide an up-to-date summary of the results of current research in their fields and give their own take on what they believe are the most significant debates influencing research, drawing original conclusions.

Cambridge Elements $\equiv$

The Philosophy of Mathematics

Elements in the Series

Paraconsistency in Mathematics
Zach Weber

Mathematical Anti-Realism and Modal Nothingism
Mark Balaguer

Plato Was Not a Mathematical Platonist
Elaine Landry

Mathematics and Explanation
Christopher Pincock

Indispensability
A. C. Paseau and Alan Baker

Lakatos and the Historical Approach to Philosophy of Mathematics
Donald Gillies

Phenomenology and Mathematics
Michael Roubach

Philosophical Uses of Categoricity Arguments
Penelope Maddy and Jouko Väänänen

Number Concepts
Richard Samuels and Eric Snyder

The Euclidean Programme
A. C. Paseau and Wesley Wrigley

Mathematical Rigour and Informal Proof
Fenner Stanley Tanswell

Mathematical Pluralism
Graham Priest

A full series listing is available at: www.cambridge.org/EPM

Printed in the United States
by Baker & Taylor Publisher Services